Parleremo Vocabulary Supplements

Getting Around

Icelandic

by Erik Zidowecki

Parleremo Vocabulary Supplements
Getting Around
Icelandic

Copyright © 2019 by Erik Zidowecki

Published by
Scriveremo Publishing
www.scriveremo.com

Printed in the United States of America

First Printing, 2019

ISBN: 9781090865571

How to use this book

There are 200 multiple choice quizzes covering 8 different categories. Each quiz has 10 questions.

The first part of the book contains the word lists for study.

The second part contains the quizzes themselves.

The third part has the solutions to the quizzes.

The final section is a dictionary of all the words.

Use this book to supplement your language learning.

Themes in this book:
Airport, Bank, Hotel, Pharmacy,
Places, Postal, Sightseeing, Zoo

Good luck!

Airport

almennt farrými *[n]* - economy class
alþjóðlegt *[adj]* - international
að bóka *[v]* - to book
að fara um borð *[v]* - to board
að fljúga *[v]* - to fly
að hætta við *[v]* - to cancel
að lenda *[v]* - to land
að lýsa yfir *[v]* - to declare
að setjast niður *[v]* - to sit down
að stimpla inn töskur *[v]* - to check bags
að taka á loft *[v]* - to take off
að vera með sér *[v]* - to carry
aðstoðarflugmaður *[m]* - copilot
bakpoki *[m]* - rucksack
beint *[adj]* - direct
beint flug - nonstop
björgunarvesti *[n]* - life preserver
brottfararspjald *[n]* - boarding pass
brottför *[f]* - departure
farangur *[m]* - luggage
farþegi *[m]* - passenger
ferðaþjónusta *[f]* - travel agency
fljúga *[v]* - flying
flug *[n]* - flight
flugbraut *[f]* - runway
flugfreyja *[f]* - stewardess
flugmaður *[m]* - pilot
flugskýli *[n]* - hangar
flugtak *[n]* - take off
flugvél *[f]* - airplane
flugvöllur *[m]* - airport
fyrsta flokks farrými *[n]* - first class
gluggi *[m]* - window
göngubrú *[f]* - gangway
heyrnartól *[f]* - headphones
hlið *[n]* - gate

hæð *[n]* - altitude
innanlands *[adj]* - domestic
innritun *[f]* - check-in
kerra *[f]* - tray
klósett *[n]* - toilet
koma *[f]* - arrival
káeta *[f]* - cabin
land *[n]* - land
löggæslumaður *[m]* - officer
miðasala *[f]* - ticket agent
miði *[m]* - ticket
miði aðra leið - single ticket
miði báðar leiðir - round trip ticket
neyðar *[m]* - emergency
seinn *[adv]* - late
skjalataska *[f]* - suitcase
snemma *[adv]* - early
sæti *[n]* - seat
súrefni *[n]* - oxygen
tenging *[f]* - connection
tollfrjáls *[adj]* - duty-free
upplýsingar *[f]* - information
vegabréf *[n]* - passport
vængur *[m]* - wing
yfirflugfreyja *[f]* - air hostess
áfangastaður *[m]* - destination
áhöfn *[f]* - crew
ókyrrð *[f]* - turbulence
öryggishlið *[n]* - metal detector
öryggisvörður *[m]* - security
útgangur *[m]* - exit
þyngd *[f]* - weight
þyrla *[f]* - helicopter
þyrlupallur *[m]* - helipad

Bank

afgangur *[m]* - change
afgreiðslumaður *[m]* - cashier
afrit *[n]* - receipt
að borga *[v]* - to pay
að draga inn *[v]* - to cash
að fá lánað *[v]* - to borrow
að leggja inn *[v]* - to deposit
að lána *[v]* - to lend
að millifæra *[v]* - to transfer
að Skipta *[v]* - to change
að skrifa undir *[v]* - to sign
að taka út *[v]* - to withdraw
aðgangur *[m]* - account
banka reikningur *[m]* - bank account
bankastaða *[f]* - account balance
bankayfirlit *[n]* - bank statement
banki *[m]* - bank
debetkort *[n]* - debit card
dollarar *[mp]* - dollars
evrur *[fp]* - euros
ferðatékki *[m]* - travellers cheque
fjárhæð *[f]* - amount
fjármagn *[f]* - capital
færslur *[fp]* - transactions
geymsla *[f]* - vault
gjald *[n]* - fee
gjaldkeri *[m]* - teller
gjaldmiðill *[m]* - currency
gjaldmiðlaskipti *[f]* - money exchanger
gjaldmiðlavirði *[n]* - exchange rate
greiðsla *[f]* - payment
gróði *[m]* - profit
hraðbanki *[m]* - ATM
innheimta *[f]* - invoice
innlögn *[f]* - deposit
kaup *[f]* - purchase

klink *[n]* - coin
kreditkort *[n]* - credit card
lán *[n]* - loan
lánstraust *[n]* - credit
millifærsla *[f]* - funds transfer
núverandi aðgangur *[m]* - current account
peningur *[m]* - money
prósenta *[f]* - percentage
samningur *[m]* - contract
seðill *[m]* - cash
skuld *[f]* - debt
sparnaðarreikningur *[m]* - savings account
sparnaður *[m]* - savings
staða *[f]* - balance
tap *[n]* - loss
tékkabók *[f]* - chequebook
tékki *[m]* - cheque
vextir *[mp]* - interest
veðsetning *[f]* - mortgage
virði *[n]* - value
viðskiptavinur *[m]* - customer
yfirmaður *[m]* - manager
öryggiskerfi *[n]* - alarm
öryggisskápur *[m]* - safe deposit box
öryggisskápur *[m]* - safe
öryggisvörður *[m]* - guard
útgjöld *[np]* - expenses
úttekt *[f]* - withdrawal

Hotel

afgreiðsla *[f]* - checkout

borð *[n]* - table

bílskúr *[m]* - garage

bókun *[f]* - booking

dyravörður *[m]* - doorman

endurgerð *[f]* - recreation

gestamóttaka *[f]* - reception desk

gestamóttakandi *[m]* - receptionist

herbergi *[n]* - room

herbergisþjónusta *[f]* - room service

hotel *[n]* - hotel

hæð *[f]* - floor

inngangur *[m]* - entrance

internet *[n]* - internet

jarðhæð *[f]* - ground floor

klósett *[n]* - loo

koddi *[m]* - pillow

kvörtun *[f]* - complaint

leigubíll *[m]* - taxi

loftræsting *[f]* - air conditioning

lykill *[m]* - key

matsalur *[m]* - dining room

morgunmatur *[m]* - breakfast

móttaka *[f]* - lobby

reikningur *[m]* - bill

rúm *[n]* - bed

skilaboð *[f]* - message

stigar *[mp]* - staircase

stigar *[mp]* - stairs

stofa *[f]* - living room

stóll *[m]* - chair

sundlaug *[f]* - swimming pool

svalir *[m]* - balcony

svíta *[f]* - suite

teppi *[n]* - blanket

teppi *[f]* - carpet

verð *[n]* - price

vikapiltur *[m]* - bellboy

ís *[m]* - ice

útsýni *[n]* - view

Pharmacy

apótek *[n]* - pharmacy
aspirin *[n]* - aspirin
hitamælir *[m]* - thermometer
hægðalyf *[n]* - laxative
innspýting *[f]* - injection
insulin *[n]* - insulin
joð *[n]* - iodine
kortisón *[n]* - cortisone
lyf *[n]* - medicine
læknir *[m]* - pharmacist
munnskol *[n]* - dental floss
pensilín *[n]* - penicillin
plástur *[m]* - bandage
sýklalyf *[n]* - antibiotic
sýróp *[n]* - syrup
tafla *[f]* - tablet
tafla *[f]* - pill
vítamín *[n]* - vitamin

Places

Afríka - Africa
Algería - Algeria
Asía - Asia
Austurríki - Austria
Bandaríkin - United States
Belgía - Belgium
Bretland - Great Britain
Danmörk - Denmark
England - England
Evrópa - Europe
Finnland - Finland
Frakkland - France
Grikkland - Greece
Holland - Netherlands
Indland - India
Japan - Japan
Júgóslavía - Yugoslavia
Kanada - Canada
Kína - China
Lúxemborg - Luxembourg

Noregur - Norway
Norður Ameríka - North America
Nýja Sjáland - New Zealand
Portúgal - Portugal
Rússland - Russia
Skotland - Scotland
Slóvenía - Slovenia
Spánn - Spain
Suður Afríka - South Africa
Suður Ameríka - South America
Sviss - Switzerland
Svíþjóð - Sweden
Tyrkland - Turkey
Túnis - Tunisia
Wales - Wales
Ástralía - Australia
Írland - Ireland
Ísrael - Israel
Ítalía - Italy
Þýskaland - Germany

Postal

afgreiðslumaður *[m]* - clerk
að bíða *[v]* - to wait
að deila *[v]* - to post
að senda *[v]* - to send
að skrifa *[v]* - to write
boðberi *[m]* - courier
bréf *[n]* - letter
bréf *[n]* - note
bréfberi *[m]* - postman
flugpóstur *[m]* - airmail
frímerki *[n]* - postage stamp
innflutningur *[m]* - import
pakki *[m]* - package
peningasending *[f]* - money order
prentað bréf *[n]* - printed item
póstbox *[n]* - letterbox
pósthús *[n]* - post office
póstur *[m]* - post
sendandi *[m]* - sender
skráð bréf *[n]* - registered letter
svar *[n]* - reply
umslag *[n]* - envelope

Sightseeing

akur *[m]* - field
andrúmsloft *[n]* - atmosphere
engi *[n]* - meadow
eyja *[f]* - island
eyðimörk *[f]* - desert
fjall *[n]* - mountain
fjörður *[m]* - bay
flatlendi *[n]* - plain
frumskógur *[m]* - jungle
gjá *[f]* - gulf
gras *[n]* - grass
haf *[n]* - ocean
hellir *[m]* - cave
hæð *[f]* - hill
jarðskjálfti *[m]* - earthquake
landslag *[n]* - landscape
lækur *[m]* - lake
nes *[n]* - cape
náttúra *[f]* - nature
sandur *[m]* - sand
sjávarföll *[f]* - tide
sjávarströnd *[f]* - coast
sjór *[m]* - sea
skagi *[m]* - peninsula
skurður *[m]* - canal
skógur *[m]* - forest
steinn *[m]* - stone
steinn *[m]* - rock
strönd *[f]* - beach
stífla *[f]* - dam
sveit *[f]* - countryside
tjörn *[f]* - pond
umhverfi *[n]* - environment
á *[f]* - river

Zoo

apahús [n] - monkey house
api [m] - monkey
aðgangur [m] - admission
bavían [m] - baboon
beltisdýr [n] - armadillo
björn [m] - bear
blettatígur [m] - cheetah
dagdýr [adj] - diurnal
dýr [n] - animal
dýragarðsgestur [m] - zoo visitor
dýragarðsvörður [m] - zookeeper
dýragarður [m] - zoo
eitraður [adj] - poisonous
fjallaljón [n] - cougar
flóðhestur [m] - hippopotamus
froskdýr [f] - amphibian
fuglasafn [n] - aviary
fílagirðing [f] - elephant enclosure
fílahús [n] - elephant house
fíll [m] - elephant
girðing [f] - enclosing wall
glerbúr [n] - glass case
gorilla [f] - gorilla
grimmilegur [adj] - fierce
gíraffahús [n] - giraffe house
gíraffi [m] - giraffe
hjörtur [m] - gazelle
hlébarði [m] - leopard
hryggleysingjar [mp] - vertebrate

hættulegur [adj] - dangerous
jaguar [m] - jaguar
jarðneskur [adj] - terrestrial
jurtaæta [f] - herbivore
kengúra [f] - kangaroo
krókódíll [m] - alligator
krókódíll [m] - crocodile
kóalabjörn [m] - koala
ljón [n] - lion
mamaldýr [n] - mammal
mammaldýr [n] - aardvark
mauraæta [f] - anteater
nashyrningur [m] - rhinoceros
næturdýr - nocturnal
panda [f] - panda
pardusdýr [n] - panther
refur [m] - fox
rándýr [f] - carnivore
sebrahestur [m] - zebra
skriðdýr [f] - reptile
skriðdýragirðing [f] - reptile enclosure
sædýr [f] - aquatic
sædýrabúr [n] - aquarium
tegundir [fp] - species
trjábýll - arboreal
tígur [m] - tiger
utandyra búr [n] - outside cage
utandyra girðing [f] - outdoor enclosure
úlfur [m] - wolf

Welcome to the
Word Quizzes section!

For each category, there are 25 quizzes, and each quiz has 10 questions.

You must choose the best match for the word given.

Word Quiz #1 - Airport

Choose the best English word to match the Icelandic word.

1) að bóka
  a) land
  b) to carry
  c) to sit down
  d) to book

2) miði báðar leiðir
  a) wing
  b) gate
  c) round trip ticket
  d) helicopter

3) öryggisvörður
  a) arrival
  b) connection
  c) passport
  d) security

4) hæð
  a) economy class
  b) boarding pass
  c) altitude
  d) to land

5) kerra
  a) tray
  b) direct
  c) toilet
  d) security

6) flugskýli
  a) to land
  b) hangar
  c) flight
  d) cabin

7) miði
  a) window
  b) luggage
  c) boarding pass
  d) ticket

8) miði aðra leið
  a) to book
  b) single ticket
  c) land
  d) arrival

9) innanlands
  a) domestic
  b) gate
  c) check-in
  d) round trip ticket

10) farangur
  a) luggage
  b) suitcase
  c) to declare
  d) round trip ticket

Word Quiz #2 - Airport

Choose the best English word to match the Icelandic word.

1) áfangastaður
  a) direct
  b) economy class
  c) take off
  d) destination

2) flugbraut
  a) runway
  b) to cancel
  c) to land
  d) passenger

3) kerra
  a) to check bags
  b) suitcase
  c) domestic
  d) tray

4) neyðar
  a) weight
  b) emergency
  c) airport
  d) helipad

5) koma
  a) crew
  b) information
  c) oxygen
  d) arrival

6) flugvöllur
  a) to take off
  b) tray
  c) to carry
  d) airport

7) bakpoki
  a) land
  b) rucksack
  c) to book
  d) round trip ticket

8) sæti
  a) seat
  b) to check bags
  c) travel agency
  d) to carry

9) þyngd
  a) weight
  b) to carry
  c) headphones
  d) hangar

10) miði báðar leiðir
  a) round trip ticket
  b) suitcase
  c) exit
  d) seat

Word Quiz #3 - Airport

Choose the best English word to match the Icelandic word.

1) klósett
  a) take off
  b) toilet
  c) seat
  d) exit

2) upplýsingar
  a) metal detector
  b) information
  c) copilot
  d) to book

3) heyrnartól
  a) headphones
  b) officer
  c) exit
  d) wing

4) hlið
  a) information
  b) gate
  c) wing
  d) weight

5) brottför
  a) luggage
  b) departure
  c) crew
  d) toilet

6) gluggi
  a) airport
  b) window
  c) destination
  d) pilot

7) neyðar
  a) rucksack
  b) flying
  c) emergency
  d) tray

8) að lýsa yfir
  a) altitude
  b) to declare
  c) ticket agent
  d) exit

9) innritun
  a) travel agency
  b) rucksack
  c) check-in
  d) pilot

10) miði báðar leiðir
  a) life preserver
  b) tray
  c) round trip ticket
  d) domestic

Word Quiz #4 - Airport

Choose the best English word to match the Icelandic word.

1) vængur
 a) wing
 b) crew
 c) exit
 d) destination

2) gluggi
 a) metal detector
 b) life preserver
 c) window
 d) air hostess

3) þyrlupallur
 a) window
 b) oxygen
 c) to take off
 d) helipad

4) hlið
 a) tray
 b) travel agency
 c) late
 d) gate

5) vegabréf
 a) passport
 b) metal detector
 c) tray
 d) flying

6) almennt farrými
 a) economy class
 b) to declare
 c) copilot
 d) emergency

7) yfirflugfreyja
 a) security
 b) air hostess
 c) crew
 d) exit

8) öryggisvörður
 a) security
 b) gate
 c) airport
 d) domestic

9) útgangur
 a) passport
 b) exit
 c) gate
 d) duty-free

10) að taka á loft
 a) to take off
 b) departure
 c) economy class
 d) flying

Word Quiz #5 - Airport

Choose the best English word to match the Icelandic word.

1) almennt farrými
- a) economy class
- b) helicopter
- c) to sit down
- d) airplane

2) flugfreyja
- a) stewardess
- b) helipad
- c) suitcase
- d) officer

3) flugbraut
- a) runway
- b) round trip ticket
- c) late
- d) air hostess

4) beint flug
- a) land
- b) destination
- c) direct
- d) nonstop

5) að lenda
- a) late
- b) to land
- c) rucksack
- d) single ticket

6) flug
- a) wheel
- b) hangar
- c) flight
- d) duty-free

7) öryggishlið
- a) metal detector
- b) tray
- c) hangar
- d) information

8) tenging
- a) altitude
- b) runway
- c) connection
- d) round trip ticket

9) snemma
- a) tray
- b) single ticket
- c) early
- d) check-in

10) yfirflugfreyja
- a) wing
- b) oxygen
- c) air hostess
- d) boarding pass

Word Quiz #6 - Airport

Choose the best English word to match the Icelandic word.

1) miði aðra leið
  a) land
  b) to take off
  c) single ticket
  d) turbulence

2) hæð
  a) suitcase
  b) late
  c) altitude
  d) luggage

3) flugskýli
  a) pilot
  b) destination
  c) security
  d) hangar

4) upplýsingar
  a) domestic
  b) information
  c) travel agency
  d) helicopter

5) almennt farrými
  a) helicopter
  b) to check bags
  c) economy class
  d) airport

6) brottför
  a) emergency
  b) check-in
  c) departure
  d) first class

7) vængur
  a) first class
  b) wing
  c) turbulence
  d) land

8) alþjóðlegt
  a) wheel
  b) international
  c) headphones
  d) first class

9) farangur
  a) helicopter
  b) oxygen
  c) emergency
  d) luggage

10) að lenda
  a) exit
  b) emergency
  c) to land
  d) hangar

Word Quiz #7 - Airport

Choose the best English word to match the Icelandic word.

1) flugbraut
  a) first class
  b) seat
  c) security
  d) runway

2) þyrlupallur
  a) toilet
  b) to sit down
  c) helipad
  d) to fly

3) alþjóðlegt
  a) toilet
  b) international
  c) nonstop
  d) exit

4) björgunarvesti
  a) life preserver
  b) turbulence
  c) duty-free
  d) passenger

5) fyrsta flokks farrými
  a) first class
  b) gate
  c) emergency
  d) luggage

6) að hætta við
  a) to book
  b) stewardess
  c) to cancel
  d) late

7) brottför
  a) travel agency
  b) departure
  c) officer
  d) pilot

8) tollfrjáls
  a) exit
  b) duty-free
  c) wheel
  d) turbulence

9) að lýsa yfir
  a) departure
  b) to declare
  c) direct
  d) to cancel

10) að bóka
  a) to book
  b) hangar
  c) oxygen
  d) exit

Word Quiz #8 - Airport
Choose the best English word to match the Icelandic word.

1) flugvöllur
 a) to cancel
 b) airport
 c) take off
 d) wing

2) ferðaþjónusta
 a) hangar
 b) early
 c) life preserver
 d) travel agency

3) að stimpla inn töskur
 a) to check bags
 b) to fly
 c) to sit down
 d) gate

4) áhöfn
 a) toilet
 b) officer
 c) crew
 d) weight

5) fljúga
 a) to cancel
 b) gate
 c) pilot
 d) flying

6) björgunarvesti
 a) airport
 b) take off
 c) life preserver
 d) duty-free

7) þyrla
 a) to sit down
 b) hangar
 c) helicopter
 d) luggage

8) innritun
 a) flight
 b) first class
 c) check-in
 d) domestic

9) útgangur
 a) to sit down
 b) exit
 c) suitcase
 d) to land

10) tollfrjáls
 a) to carry
 b) check-in
 c) connection
 d) duty-free

Word Quiz #9 - Airport

Choose the best English word to match the Icelandic word.

1) flugskýli
 a) hangar
 b) to cancel
 c) early
 d) flying

2) brottfararspjald
 a) to board
 b) boarding pass
 c) international
 d) check-in

3) aðstoðarflugmaður
 a) copilot
 b) travel agency
 c) officer
 d) stewardess

4) alþjóðlegt
 a) life preserver
 b) headphones
 c) international
 d) airport

5) þyrla
 a) exit
 b) copilot
 c) boarding pass
 d) helicopter

6) innanlands
 a) turbulence
 b) life preserver
 c) emergency
 d) domestic

7) farþegi
 a) passenger
 b) stewardess
 c) wing
 d) information

8) land
 a) land
 b) helicopter
 c) travel agency
 d) metal detector

9) miðasala
 a) to declare
 b) tray
 c) ticket agent
 d) helipad

10) að bóka
 a) exit
 b) round trip ticket
 c) information
 d) to book

Word Quiz #10 - Airport

Choose the best English word to match the Icelandic word.

1) klósett
 a) toilet
 b) to land
 c) to take off
 d) airplane

2) alþjóðlegt
 a) metal detector
 b) early
 c) international
 d) duty-free

3) göngubrú
 a) round trip ticket
 b) to fly
 c) gangway
 d) airport

4) beint flug
 a) single ticket
 b) rucksack
 c) nonstop
 d) seat

5) farþegi
 a) luggage
 b) suitcase
 c) metal detector
 d) passenger

6) hlið
 a) to board
 b) cabin
 c) gate
 d) direct

7) seinn
 a) flying
 b) late
 c) window
 d) gangway

8) þyngd
 a) direct
 b) weight
 c) gate
 d) window

9) upplýsingar
 a) direct
 b) tray
 c) information
 d) to carry

10) að fljúga
 a) duty-free
 b) to fly
 c) travel agency
 d) late

Word Quiz #11 - Airport

Choose the best English word to match the Icelandic word.

1) sæti
 a) officer
 b) seat
 c) weight
 d) metal detector

2) tenging
 a) connection
 b) late
 c) to board
 d) to book

3) þyngd
 a) weight
 b) oxygen
 c) headphones
 d) wheel

4) innanlands
 a) tray
 b) wheel
 c) domestic
 d) late

5) aðstoðarflugmaður
 a) boarding pass
 b) emergency
 c) nonstop
 d) copilot

6) flug
 a) flight
 b) wing
 c) passport
 d) hangar

7) miði
 a) ticket
 b) single ticket
 c) to take off
 d) information

8) björgunarvesti
 a) destination
 b) oxygen
 c) ticket
 d) life preserver

9) tollfrjáls
 a) security
 b) duty-free
 c) seat
 d) ticket

10) miðasala
 a) turbulence
 b) metal detector
 c) tray
 d) ticket agent

Word Quiz #12 - Airport

Choose the best English word to match the Icelandic word.

1) almennt farrými
a) duty-free
b) tray
c) headphones
d) economy class

2) að lenda
a) to fly
b) ticket
c) helicopter
d) to land

3) að vera með sér
a) wheel
b) to carry
c) hangar
d) first class

4) tollfrjáls
a) to book
b) wheel
c) duty-free
d) exit

5) farangur
a) luggage
b) copilot
c) exit
d) to sit down

6) bakpoki
a) information
b) rucksack
c) tray
d) flying

7) flugfreyja
a) life preserver
b) luggage
c) stewardess
d) nonstop

8) að stimpla inn töskur
a) rucksack
b) copilot
c) to check bags
d) pilot

9) gluggi
a) destination
b) window
c) check-in
d) weight

10) miði báðar leiðir
a) round trip ticket
b) passenger
c) airport
d) early

Word Quiz #13 - Airport

Choose the best English word to match the Icelandic word.

1) tollfrjáls
a) stewardess
b) duty-free
c) wing
d) information

2) þyrla
a) ticket agent
b) helicopter
c) early
d) wing

3) miði
a) arrival
b) air hostess
c) ticket
d) take off

4) miði báðar leiðir
a) arrival
b) take off
c) tray
d) round trip ticket

5) klósett
a) toilet
b) check-in
c) direct
d) round trip ticket

6) þyngd
a) weight
b) altitude
c) air hostess
d) destination

7) sæti
a) domestic
b) seat
c) helicopter
d) hangar

8) flugtak
a) helipad
b) cabin
c) take off
d) hangar

9) að stimpla inn töskur
a) turbulence
b) destination
c) to take off
d) to check bags

10) upplýsingar
a) first class
b) duty-free
c) information
d) officer

Word Quiz #14 - Airport

Choose the best Icelandic word to match the English word.

1) round trip ticket
a) hæð
b) hlið
c) land
d) miði báðar leiðir

2) arrival
a) súrefni
b) að hætta við
c) koma
d) miði aðra leið

3) early
a) snemma
b) innanlands
c) land
d) farþegi

4) security
a) að fara um borð
b) áhöfn
c) flugskýli
d) öryggisvörður

5) to carry
a) að vera með sér
b) upplýsingar
c) súrefni
d) innanlands

6) airport
a) að setjast niður
b) flugvöllur
c) koma
d) snemma

7) to take off
a) seinn
b) að taka á loft
c) flugbraut
d) koma

8) to declare
a) brottför
b) að lýsa yfir
c) þyrla
d) áfangastaður

9) hangar
a) útgangur
b) flugskýli
c) beint flug
d) flug

10) luggage
a) farangur
b) hjól
c) aðstoðarflugmaður
d) að bóka

Word Quiz #15 - Airport

Choose the best Icelandic word to match the English word.

1) to declare
 a) flugtak
 b) kerra
 c) fljúga
 d) að lýsa yfir

2) economy class
 a) að setjast niður
 b) þyngd
 c) almennt farrými
 d) neyðar

3) helipad
 a) að lýsa yfir
 b) flugtak
 c) björgunarvesti
 d) þyrlupallur

4) copilot
 a) aðstoðarflugmaður
 b) beint
 c) hæð
 d) flugmaður

5) security
 a) þyngd
 b) öryggisvörður
 c) útgangur
 d) alþjóðlegt

6) early
 a) klósett
 b) að bóka
 c) miði
 d) snemma

7) international
 a) klósett
 b) sæti
 c) alþjóðlegt
 d) farþegi

8) life preserver
 a) tenging
 b) björgunarvesti
 c) að bóka
 d) tollfrjáls

9) nonstop
 a) flugbraut
 b) beint flug
 c) gluggi
 d) flugfreyja

10) runway
 a) flugmaður
 b) flugbraut
 c) miði báðar leiðir
 d) þyngd

Word Quiz #16 - Airport

Choose the best Icelandic word to match the English word.

1) first class
- a) snemma
- b) neyðar
- c) öryggisvörður
- d) fyrsta flokks farrými

2) pilot
- a) flugmaður
- b) að bóka
- c) flugvél
- d) alþjóðlegt

3) seat
- a) útgangur
- b) sæti
- c) að setjast niður
- d) káeta

4) early
- a) að lenda
- b) snemma
- c) útgangur
- d) þyngd

5) passenger
- a) koma
- b) káeta
- c) að bóka
- d) farþegi

6) rucksack
- a) neyðar
- b) beint
- c) koma
- d) bakpoki

7) toilet
- a) fyrsta flokks farrými
- b) flugbraut
- c) yfirflugfreyja
- d) klósett

8) domestic
- a) áhöfn
- b) innanlands
- c) neyðar
- d) almennt farrými

9) flying
- a) flugvöllur
- b) fljúga
- c) beint
- d) flugmaður

10) oxygen
- a) vegabréf
- b) klósett
- c) súrefni
- d) áfangastaður

Word Quiz #17 - Airport

Choose the best Icelandic word to match the English word.

1) destination
 a) flugfreyja
 b) áfangastaður
 c) flugvöllur
 d) brottfararspjald

2) gangway
 a) að hætta við
 b) göngubrú
 c) flugvél
 d) að vera með sér

3) ticket agent
 a) yfirflugfreyja
 b) miðasala
 c) brottför
 d) ferðaþjónusta

4) altitude
 a) neyðar
 b) flugmaður
 c) snemma
 d) hæð

5) connection
 a) farþegi
 b) þyrla
 c) gluggi
 d) tenging

6) to sit down
 a) að setjast niður
 b) að lenda
 c) að fljúga
 d) upplýsingar

7) toilet
 a) klósett
 b) áfangastaður
 c) ferðaþjónusta
 d) að lýsa yfir

8) flight
 a) flug
 b) göngubrú
 c) heyrnartól
 d) koma

9) exit
 a) þyngd
 b) seinn
 c) upplýsingar
 d) útgangur

10) travel agency
 a) súrefni
 b) ferðaþjónusta
 c) tenging
 d) björgunarvesti

Word Quiz #18 - Airport

Choose the best Icelandic word to match the English word.

1) destination
 a) neyðar
 b) björgunarvesti
 c) hæð
 d) áfangastaður

2) pilot
 a) að vera með sér
 b) göngubrú
 c) súrefni
 d) flugmaður

3) to fly
 a) flugvél
 b) miði aðra leið
 c) að fljúga
 d) miðasala

4) headphones
 a) þyrla
 b) heyrnartól
 c) miði aðra leið
 d) flug

5) take off
 a) flugtak
 b) flugmaður
 c) að lýsa yfir
 d) áhöfn

6) weight
 a) að stimpla inn töskur
 b) þyngd
 c) að taka á loft
 d) útgangur

7) suitcase
 a) flugvöllur
 b) kerra
 c) að lenda
 d) skjalataska

8) to sit down
 a) hæð
 b) miðasala
 c) beint flug
 d) að setjast niður

9) flying
 a) að vera með sér
 b) innritun
 c) kerra
 d) fljúga

10) hangar
 a) löggæslumaður
 b) áhöfn
 c) flugskýli
 d) almennt farrými

Word Quiz #19 - Airport

Choose the best Icelandic word to match the English word.

1) to check bags
 a) löggæslumaður
 b) gluggi
 c) súrefni
 d) að stimpla inn töskur

2) headphones
 a) heyrnartól
 b) öryggishlið
 c) björgunarvesti
 d) brottfararspjald

3) direct
 a) beint
 b) beint flug
 c) ókyrrð
 d) miði báðar leiðir

4) airplane
 a) yfirflugfreyja
 b) skjalataska
 c) áfangastaður
 d) flugvél

5) copilot
 a) aðstoðarflugmaður
 b) löggæslumaður
 c) gluggi
 d) flugskýli

6) seat
 a) að fljúga
 b) ferðaþjónusta
 c) sæti
 d) vængur

7) officer
 a) neyðar
 b) að fara um borð
 c) miðasala
 d) löggæslumaður

8) rucksack
 a) ferðaþjónusta
 b) bakpoki
 c) að lenda
 d) almennt farrými

9) suitcase
 a) áfangastaður
 b) almennt farrými
 c) að taka á loft
 d) skjalataska

10) duty-free
 a) fljúga
 b) land
 c) tollfrjáls
 d) neyðar

Word Quiz #20 - Airport

Choose the best Icelandic word to match the English word.

1) single ticket
a) löggæslumaður
b) miðasala
c) miði aðra leið
d) gluggi

2) tray
a) útgangur
b) flugskýli
c) heyrnartól
d) kerra

3) arrival
a) brottför
b) ókyrrð
c) klósett
d) koma

4) information
a) að fljúga
b) flug
c) vegabréf
d) upplýsingar

5) wheel
a) að vera með sér
b) land
c) súrefni
d) hjól

6) life preserver
a) brottfararspjald
b) björgunarvesti
c) innanlands
d) miði báðar leiðir

7) seat
a) sæti
b) aðstoðarflugmaður
c) yfirflugfreyja
d) miði báðar leiðir

8) runway
a) flugbraut
b) klósett
c) að fara um borð
d) að setjast niður

9) connection
a) að setjast niður
b) þyngd
c) heyrnartól
d) tenging

10) airplane
a) seinn
b) björgunarvesti
c) flugvél
d) hjól

Word Quiz #21 - Airport

Choose the best Icelandic word to match the English word.

1) helicopter
  a) flugskýli
  b) þyrlupallur
  c) þyrla
  d) að lenda

2) domestic
  a) súrefni
  b) að hætta við
  c) seinn
  d) innanlands

3) to fly
  a) flugfreyja
  b) áhöfn
  c) vængur
  d) að fljúga

4) departure
  a) fyrsta flokks farrými
  b) almennt farrými
  c) brottför
  d) að hætta við

5) destination
  a) áfangastaður
  b) björgunarvesti
  c) sæti
  d) að vera með sér

6) single ticket
  a) miði aðra leið
  b) flugvél
  c) hæð
  d) löggæslumaður

7) round trip ticket
  a) flugvöllur
  b) miði
  c) vængur
  d) miði báðar leiðir

8) to sit down
  a) flugskýli
  b) að setjast niður
  c) miði aðra leið
  d) farþegi

9) wing
  a) að stimpla inn töskur
  b) vængur
  c) fljúga
  d) bakpoki

10) life preserver
  a) björgunarvesti
  b) flugmaður
  c) klósett
  d) miði aðra leið

Word Quiz #22 - Airport

Choose the best Icelandic word to match the English word.

1) airport
a) kerra
b) flugvöllur
c) áhöfn
d) snemma

2) helipad
a) áfangastaður
b) land
c) útgangur
d) þyrlupallur

3) to declare
a) hjól
b) miði
c) súrefni
d) að lýsa yfir

4) life preserver
a) upplýsingar
b) björgunarvesti
c) almennt farrými
d) útgangur

5) to cancel
a) að hætta við
b) öryggishlið
c) að setjast niður
d) áfangastaður

6) exit
a) gluggi
b) flugskýli
c) ókyrrð
d) útgangur

7) to book
a) að fara um borð
b) tenging
c) farþegi
d) að bóka

8) boarding pass
a) miði
b) beint flug
c) gluggi
d) brottfararspjald

9) altitude
a) björgunarvesti
b) útgangur
c) hæð
d) brottfararspjald

10) travel agency
a) hjól
b) öryggisvörður
c) land
d) ferðaþjónusta

Word Quiz #23 - Airport

Choose the best Icelandic word to match the English word.

1) economy class
 a) flugvöllur
 b) gluggi
 c) beint flug
 d) almennt farrými

2) to land
 a) ferðaþjónusta
 b) klósett
 c) að lenda
 d) að setjast niður

3) take off
 a) þyrlupallur
 b) flugtak
 c) alþjóðlegt
 d) hæð

4) flying
 a) farþegi
 b) þyrlupallur
 c) hjól
 d) fljúga

5) gangway
 a) alþjóðlegt
 b) ferðaþjónusta
 c) almennt farrými
 d) göngubrú

6) to take off
 a) ókyrrð
 b) alþjóðlegt
 c) öryggisvörður
 d) að taka á loft

7) direct
 a) beint
 b) göngubrú
 c) flugvél
 d) snemma

8) rucksack
 a) snemma
 b) þyrlupallur
 c) bakpoki
 d) farangur

9) crew
 a) farangur
 b) almennt farrými
 c) að stimpla inn töskur
 d) áhöfn

10) ticket agent
 a) áhöfn
 b) miðasala
 c) innanlands
 d) flugbraut

Word Quiz #24 - Airport

Choose the best Icelandic word to match the English word.

1) altitude
a) að stimpla inn töskur
b) hæð
c) flugvöllur
d) ókyrrð

2) to book
a) beint flug
b) þyrla
c) að bóka
d) flugfreyja

3) early
a) snemma
b) klósett
c) vængur
d) vegabréf

4) nonstop
a) bakpoki
b) sæti
c) klósett
d) beint flug

5) international
a) seinn
b) káeta
c) alþjóðlegt
d) að hætta við

6) land
a) vængur
b) klósett
c) fljúga
d) land

7) late
a) hæð
b) seinn
c) þyngd
d) miði báðar leiðir

8) exit
a) farangur
b) útgangur
c) að lenda
d) að setjast niður

9) helicopter
a) björgunarvesti
b) þyrla
c) að setjast niður
d) upplýsingar

10) to take off
a) súrefni
b) að taka á loft
c) almennt farrými
d) útgangur

Word Quiz #25 - Airport

Choose the best Icelandic word to match the English word.

1) to check bags
a) að stimpla inn töskur
b) heyrnartól
c) að fljúga
d) áfangastaður

2) exit
a) útgangur
b) að stimpla inn töskur
c) súrefni
d) að lenda

3) late
a) seinn
b) miði aðra leið
c) innritun
d) flugfreyja

4) ticket
a) miði
b) neyðar
c) að lýsa yfir
d) seinn

5) to cancel
a) að hætta við
b) að fljúga
c) skjalataska
d) koma

6) airplane
a) að hætta við
b) vegabréf
c) flugvél
d) útgangur

7) stewardess
a) öryggishlið
b) flugfreyja
c) gluggi
d) alþjóðlegt

8) passport
a) yfirflugfreyja
b) flugbraut
c) vegabréf
d) beint

9) to declare
a) innritun
b) þyrla
c) að lýsa yfir
d) farþegi

10) single ticket
a) vegabréf
b) flugmaður
c) miði aðra leið
d) fyrsta flokks farrými

Word Quiz #26 - Bank

Choose the best English word to match the Icelandic word.

1) sparnaðarreikningur
  a) alarm
  b) transactions
  c) savings account
  d) coin

2) sparnaður
  a) savings
  b) manager
  c) travellers cheque
  d) amount

3) ferðatékki
  a) euros
  b) account balance
  c) currency
  d) travellers cheque

4) banka reikningur
  a) bank account
  b) contract
  c) receipt
  d) percentage

5) greiðsla
  a) amount
  b) cashier
  c) safe
  d) payment

6) gróði
  a) amount
  b) funds transfer
  c) profit
  d) manager

7) að leggja inn
  a) customer
  b) savings
  c) cheque
  d) to deposit

8) núverandi aðgangur
  a) current account
  b) exchange rate
  c) bank statement
  d) to withdraw

9) hlutabréf
  a) current account
  b) share
  c) safe deposit box
  d) contract

10) öryggiskerfi
  a) value
  b) money exchanger
  c) share
  d) alarm

Word Quiz #27 - Bank

Choose the best English word to match the Icelandic word.

1) öryggisskápur
 a) purchase
 b) to change
 c) safe deposit box
 d) teller

2) hlutabréf
 a) amount
 b) chequebook
 c) loss
 d) share

3) gjaldmiðlavirði
 a) currency
 b) exchange rate
 c) balance
 d) fee

4) samningur
 a) percentage
 b) bank account
 c) teller
 d) contract

5) gróði
 a) transactions
 b) percentage
 c) profit
 d) change

6) að skrifa undir
 a) fee
 b) value
 c) coin
 d) to sign

7) peningur
 a) cheque
 b) manager
 c) money
 d) to withdraw

8) öryggisvörður
 a) loan
 b) change
 c) guard
 d) withdrawal

9) banka reikningur
 a) percentage
 b) safe deposit box
 c) to borrow
 d) bank account

10) viðskiptavinur
 a) cash
 b) customer
 c) percentage
 d) debt

Word Quiz #28 - Bank

Choose the best English word to match the Icelandic word.

1) aðgangur
a) dollars
b) teller
c) account
d) deposit

2) prósenta
a) profit
b) chequebook
c) capital
d) percentage

3) peningur
a) to withdraw
b) money
c) safe
d) profit

4) bankastaða
a) money
b) cash
c) account balance
d) current account

5) vextir
a) percentage
b) interest
c) value
d) account

6) kreditkort
a) account balance
b) credit card
c) debt
d) money exchanger

7) evrur
a) safe deposit box
b) contract
c) savings
d) euros

8) millifærsla
a) funds transfer
b) to transfer
c) percentage
d) safe

9) dollarar
a) loan
b) dollars
c) debt
d) debit card

10) að Skipta
a) safe
b) to change
c) bank
d) payment

Word Quiz #29 - Bank

Choose the best English word to match the Icelandic word.

1) fjárhæð
 a) cashier
 b) savings account
 c) manager
 d) amount

2) innlögn
 a) withdrawal
 b) to cash
 c) deposit
 d) debt

3) gjaldmiðlavirði
 a) manager
 b) exchange rate
 c) invoice
 d) loss

4) hraðbanki
 a) mortgage
 b) ATM
 c) alarm
 d) capital

5) sparnaðarreikningur
 a) savings account
 b) change
 c) to cash
 d) payment

6) úttekt
 a) withdrawal
 b) cash
 c) to pay
 d) credit

7) gróði
 a) contract
 b) teller
 c) profit
 d) loan

8) viðskiptavinur
 a) savings
 b) customer
 c) profit
 d) invoice

9) bankayfirlit
 a) fee
 b) bank account
 c) bank statement
 d) travellers cheque

10) að lána
 a) debt
 b) to lend
 c) deposit
 d) loss

Word Quiz #30 - Bank

Choose the best English word to match the Icelandic word.

1) að borga
 a) to pay
 b) to withdraw
 c) account balance
 d) savings account

2) tékki
 a) cashier
 b) cheque
 c) currency
 d) balance

3) gjaldmiðlavirði
 a) invoice
 b) travellers cheque
 c) profit
 d) exchange rate

4) bankastaða
 a) teller
 b) cashier
 c) account balance
 d) to deposit

5) lánstraust
 a) invoice
 b) to withdraw
 c) expenses
 d) credit

6) gróði
 a) credit card
 b) profit
 c) to sign
 d) capital

7) seðill
 a) cash
 b) money exchanger
 c) cheque
 d) to transfer

8) innheimta
 a) money
 b) invoice
 c) coin
 d) to cash

9) færslur
 a) payment
 b) transactions
 c) purchase
 d) coin

10) að fá lánað
 a) to borrow
 b) payment
 c) profit
 d) cheque

Word Quiz #31 - Bank

Choose the best English word to match the Icelandic word.

1) klink
 a) credit
 b) euros
 c) account
 d) coin

2) yfirmaður
 a) cashier
 b) manager
 c) funds transfer
 d) vault

3) að skrifa undir
 a) to sign
 b) withdrawal
 c) coin
 d) profit

4) gjaldmiðlavirði
 a) exchange rate
 b) account
 c) teller
 d) interest

5) úttekt
 a) to pay
 b) withdrawal
 c) debt
 d) contract

6) lán
 a) travellers cheque
 b) cash
 c) loan
 d) ATM

7) debetkort
 a) debit card
 b) to sign
 c) transactions
 d) to change

8) að millifæra
 a) ATM
 b) vault
 c) to borrow
 d) to transfer

9) banki
 a) to transfer
 b) to cash
 c) bank
 d) deposit

10) að lána
 a) contract
 b) to lend
 c) safe
 d) currency

Word Quiz #32 - Bank

Choose the best English word to match the Icelandic word.

1) banki
  a) funds transfer
  b) bank
  c) expenses
  d) amount

2) tékkabók
  a) vault
  b) loss
  c) chequebook
  d) balance

3) vextir
  a) euros
  b) teller
  c) cashier
  d) interest

4) hlutabréf
  a) alarm
  b) share
  c) bank statement
  d) money exchanger

5) gjaldmiðill
  a) to borrow
  b) currency
  c) exchange rate
  d) account

6) lán
  a) receipt
  b) loan
  c) deposit
  d) change

7) innlögn
  a) deposit
  b) purchase
  c) to cash
  d) teller

8) gjald
  a) to sign
  b) fee
  c) deposit
  d) to withdraw

9) peningur
  a) safe
  b) money
  c) credit card
  d) funds transfer

10) geymsla
  a) cash
  b) expenses
  c) alarm
  d) vault

Word Quiz #33 - Bank

Choose the best English word to match the Icelandic word.

1) staða
a) invoice
b) balance
c) loan
d) credit card

2) viðskiptavinur
a) teller
b) transactions
c) currency
d) customer

3) bankastaða
a) guard
b) account balance
c) receipt
d) ATM

4) sparnaðarreikningur
a) loss
b) amount
c) safe deposit box
d) savings account

5) skuld
a) change
b) debt
c) to sign
d) vault

6) fjárhæð
a) amount
b) contract
c) cashier
d) to transfer

7) að fá lánað
a) funds transfer
b) contract
c) to borrow
d) to pay

8) banki
a) to pay
b) bank
c) cash
d) to borrow

9) yfirmaður
a) capital
b) chequebook
c) debt
d) manager

10) úttekt
a) withdrawal
b) travellers cheque
c) customer
d) debit card

Word Quiz #34 - Bank

Choose the best English word to match the Icelandic word.

1) að fá lánað
   a) to borrow
   b) travellers cheque
   c) capital
   d) share

2) vextir
   a) ATM
   b) interest
   c) purchase
   d) savings

3) prósenta
   a) change
   b) percentage
   c) invoice
   d) euros

4) peningur
   a) loss
   b) to cash
   c) mortgage
   d) money

5) sparnaðarreikningur
   a) manager
   b) vault
   c) cheque
   d) savings account

6) kaup
   a) amount
   b) safe deposit box
   c) capital
   d) purchase

7) seðill
   a) euros
   b) deposit
   c) cash
   d) travellers cheque

8) dollarar
   a) travellers cheque
   b) credit card
   c) dollars
   d) credit

9) evrur
   a) teller
   b) euros
   c) profit
   d) to pay

10) ferðatékki
   a) safe
   b) teller
   c) bank account
   d) travellers cheque

Word Quiz #35 - Bank

Choose the best English word to match the Icelandic word.

1) afgangur
   a) bank
   b) share
   c) change
   d) guard

2) að skrifa undir
   a) account balance
   b) to cash
   c) to sign
   d) cash

3) útgjöld
   a) expenses
   b) invoice
   c) cash
   d) savings

4) lánstraust
   a) profit
   b) chequebook
   c) to pay
   d) credit

5) greiðsla
   a) coin
   b) savings account
   c) deposit
   d) payment

6) að leggja inn
   a) euros
   b) to deposit
   c) debit card
   d) current account

7) geymsla
   a) debt
   b) expenses
   c) vault
   d) purchase

8) öryggisvörður
   a) guard
   b) amount
   c) teller
   d) capital

9) lán
   a) payment
   b) to change
   c) loan
   d) interest

10) yfirmaður
   a) coin
   b) funds transfer
   c) manager
   d) bank

Word Quiz #36 - Bank

Choose the best English word to match the Icelandic word.

1) öryggisskápur
 a) safe
 b) contract
 c) cash
 d) savings

2) afgreiðslumaður
 a) savings
 b) deposit
 c) cashier
 d) account

3) tap
 a) to borrow
 b) dollars
 c) loss
 d) to withdraw

4) að taka út
 a) to withdraw
 b) receipt
 c) account
 d) contract

5) gjaldmiðlavirði
 a) receipt
 b) transactions
 c) exchange rate
 d) credit card

6) kreditkort
 a) cashier
 b) mortgage
 c) credit card
 d) savings account

7) að millifæra
 a) safe deposit box
 b) to transfer
 c) account balance
 d) to pay

8) prósenta
 a) debt
 b) percentage
 c) savings account
 d) to pay

9) að borga
 a) savings
 b) to pay
 c) profit
 d) guard

10) sparnaður
 a) account
 b) credit
 c) cash
 d) savings

Word Quiz #37 - Bank

Choose the best English word to match the Icelandic word.

1) banki
  a) bank statement
  b) interest
  c) bank
  d) guard

2) gróði
  a) bank account
  b) mortgage
  c) profit
  d) amount

3) afgreiðslumaður
  a) bank statement
  b) fee
  c) cashier
  d) withdrawal

4) millifærsla
  a) account
  b) to sign
  c) to deposit
  d) funds transfer

5) fjármagn
  a) currency
  b) interest
  c) savings account
  d) capital

6) evrur
  a) euros
  b) receipt
  c) guard
  d) payment

7) yfirmaður
  a) travellers cheque
  b) cash
  c) manager
  d) current account

8) að taka út
  a) manager
  b) to change
  c) bank
  d) to withdraw

9) virði
  a) value
  b) interest
  c) receipt
  d) teller

10) sparnaður
  a) travellers cheque
  b) savings
  c) manager
  d) to pay

Word Quiz #38 - Bank

Choose the best English word to match the Icelandic word.

1) afgreiðslumaður
  a) expenses
  b) to change
  c) amount
  d) cashier

2) tékki
  a) account balance
  b) cheque
  c) customer
  d) interest

3) öryggisvörður
  a) to withdraw
  b) exchange rate
  c) guard
  d) cash

4) að lána
  a) to lend
  b) to transfer
  c) to withdraw
  d) transactions

5) innheimta
  a) to withdraw
  b) money
  c) invoice
  d) ATM

6) úttekt
  a) expenses
  b) withdrawal
  c) teller
  d) transactions

7) banki
  a) bank statement
  b) payment
  c) bank
  d) receipt

8) tap
  a) profit
  b) loss
  c) teller
  d) to deposit

9) debetkort
  a) account balance
  b) cheque
  c) debit card
  d) expenses

10) núverandi aðgangur
  a) loss
  b) current account
  c) payment
  d) interest

Word Quiz #39 - Bank

Choose the best Icelandic word to match the English word.

1) capital
  a) fjármagn
  b) bankayfirlit
  c) veðsetning
  d) að Skipta

2) savings
  a) millifærsla
  b) færslur
  c) tap
  d) sparnaður

3) account balance
  a) gjaldmiðlaskipti
  b) bankastaða
  c) lán
  d) seðill

4) currency
  a) seðill
  b) hraðbanki
  c) evrur
  d) gjaldmiðill

5) funds transfer
  a) millifærsla
  b) yfirmaður
  c) sparnaðarreikningur
  d) úttekt

6) invoice
  a) gjaldmiðlaskipti
  b) fjárhæð
  c) öryggisskápur
  d) innheimta

7) to cash
  a) bankastaða
  b) peningur
  c) að draga inn
  d) úttekt

8) savings account
  a) gjaldmiðill
  b) sparnaðarreikningur
  c) banki
  d) núverandi aðgangur

9) balance
  a) að fá lánað
  b) evrur
  c) staða
  d) geymsla

10) safe deposit box
  a) öryggisskápur
  b) vextir
  c) greiðsla
  d) að fá lánað

Word Quiz #40 - Bank

Choose the best Icelandic word to match the English word.

1) expenses
 a) útgjöld
 b) gróði
 c) debetkort
 d) seðill

2) exchange rate
 a) gjaldmiðlavirði
 b) að Skipta
 c) sparnaðarreikningur
 d) sparnaður

3) debt
 a) vextir
 b) aðgangur
 c) skuld
 d) hlutabréf

4) current account
 a) núverandi aðgangur
 b) yfirmaður
 c) banki
 d) gjald

5) vault
 a) að leggja inn
 b) geymsla
 c) öryggisvörður
 d) gróði

6) money exchanger
 a) öryggisvörður
 b) gjaldmiðlaskipti
 c) vextir
 d) bankastaða

7) contract
 a) evrur
 b) samningur
 c) gróði
 d) að borga

8) transactions
 a) banki
 b) kaup
 c) færslur
 d) að borga

9) safe
 a) að taka út
 b) tap
 c) sparnaður
 d) öryggisskápur

10) capital
 a) fjármagn
 b) öryggiskerfi
 c) sparnaðarreikningur
 d) að skrifa undir

Word Quiz #41 - Bank

Choose the best Icelandic word to match the English word.

1) loss
  a) ferðatékki
  b) evrur
  c) tap
  d) dollarar

2) profit
  a) gróði
  b) hlutabréf
  c) klink
  d) að skrifa undir

3) to sign
  a) lán
  b) afrit
  c) að skrifa undir
  d) að taka út

4) interest
  a) vextir
  b) peningur
  c) bankayfirlit
  d) prósenta

5) safe
  a) lánstraust
  b) öryggisskápur
  c) yfirmaður
  d) geymsla

6) savings account
  a) sparnaðarreikningur
  b) innlögn
  c) klink
  d) úttekt

7) share
  a) gjaldkeri
  b) úttekt
  c) sparnaður
  d) hlutabréf

8) ATM
  a) hraðbanki
  b) veðsetning
  c) færslur
  d) að skrifa undir

9) to cash
  a) vextir
  b) gjaldkeri
  c) að draga inn
  d) hraðbanki

10) account balance
  a) að millifæra
  b) innlögn
  c) klink
  d) bankastaða

Word Quiz #42 - Bank

Choose the best Icelandic word to match the English word.

1) balance
   a) lán
   b) staða
   c) afgreiðslumaður
   d) tékki

2) change
   a) samningur
   b) afgangur
   c) lán
   d) gjaldmiðlavirði

3) guard
   a) öryggisskápur
   b) öryggisvörður
   c) gjaldmiðlavirði
   d) veðsetning

4) to transfer
   a) evrur
   b) virði
   c) samningur
   d) að millifæra

5) account
   a) sparnaðarreikningur
   b) aðgangur
   c) gjaldmiðlaskipti
   d) að draga inn

6) deposit
   a) peningur
   b) tékki
   c) hlutabréf
   d) innlögn

7) savings account
   a) aðgangur
   b) klink
   c) kreditkort
   d) sparnaðarreikningur

8) capital
   a) kreditkort
   b) öryggisskápur
   c) skuld
   d) fjármagn

9) money
   a) evrur
   b) að fá lánað
   c) núverandi aðgangur
   d) peningur

10) value
   a) tékki
   b) tékkabók
   c) virði
   d) banki

Word Quiz #43 - Bank

Choose the best Icelandic word to match the English word.

1) to borrow
 a) tékkabók
 b) úttekt
 c) debetkort
 d) að fá lánað

2) bank statement
 a) að draga inn
 b) afrit
 c) öryggisskápur
 d) bankayfirlit

3) loss
 a) að draga inn
 b) tap
 c) greiðsla
 d) prósenta

4) credit
 a) að millifæra
 b) kaup
 c) lánstraust
 d) bankastaða

5) to change
 a) afgangur
 b) að fá lánað
 c) að Skipta
 d) viðskiptavinur

6) account balance
 a) kaup
 b) bankastaða
 c) hlutabréf
 d) millifærsla

7) dollars
 a) dollarar
 b) geymsla
 c) lánstraust
 d) innheimta

8) profit
 a) gróði
 b) að millifæra
 c) sparnaðarreikningur
 d) hlutabréf

9) credit card
 a) yfirmaður
 b) hraðbanki
 c) tap
 d) kreditkort

10) to sign
 a) innheimta
 b) að skrifa undir
 c) sparnaðarreikningur
 d) lán

Word Quiz #44 - Bank

Choose the best Icelandic word to match the English word.

1) capital
a) geymsla
b) gjaldmiðlaskipti
c) kaup
d) fjármagn

2) savings
a) að fá lánað
b) gjald
c) sparnaður
d) prósenta

3) amount
a) fjárhæð
b) seðill
c) gjaldmiðlavirði
d) að skrifa undir

4) travellers cheque
a) úttekt
b) geymsla
c) gjald
d) ferðatékki

5) dollars
a) dollarar
b) gjaldkeri
c) millifærsla
d) lánstraust

6) currency
a) úttekt
b) útgjöld
c) gjaldmiðill
d) seðill

7) withdrawal
a) úttekt
b) prósenta
c) kreditkort
d) gróði

8) vault
a) gjaldmiðlavirði
b) geymsla
c) öryggisvörður
d) yfirmaður

9) cashier
a) afgreiðslumaður
b) öryggiskerfi
c) núverandi aðgangur
d) hraðbanki

10) bank
a) banki
b) gjaldkeri
c) lán
d) öryggisvörður

Word Quiz #45 - Bank

Choose the best Icelandic word to match the English word.

1) money exchanger
  a) gjaldmiðlaskipti
  b) núverandi aðgangur
  c) evrur
  d) afrit

2) vault
  a) evrur
  b) geymsla
  c) viðskiptavinur
  d) sparnaðarreikningur

3) currency
  a) að borga
  b) að fá lánað
  c) útgjöld
  d) gjaldmiðill

4) alarm
  a) staða
  b) öryggiskerfi
  c) afrit
  d) tékkabók

5) cash
  a) að skrifa undir
  b) afgangur
  c) seðill
  d) yfirmaður

6) balance
  a) aðgangur
  b) að borga
  c) staða
  d) hlutabréf

7) to lend
  a) innlögn
  b) gjald
  c) að lána
  d) gjaldmiðlaskipti

8) loss
  a) tap
  b) aðgangur
  c) sparnaður
  d) peningur

9) funds transfer
  a) innlögn
  b) millifærsla
  c) sparnaður
  d) kreditkort

10) money
  a) viðskiptavinur
  b) dollarar
  c) hlutabréf
  d) peningur

Word Quiz #46 - Bank

Choose the best Icelandic word to match the English word.

1) change
   a) millifærsla
   b) afgangur
   c) kreditkort
   d) lán

2) bank
   a) seðill
   b) banki
   c) öryggisskápur
   d) fjárhæð

3) teller
   a) afgreiðslumaður
   b) bankayfirlit
   c) kreditkort
   d) gjaldkeri

4) percentage
   a) gjaldmiðill
   b) innheimta
   c) prósenta
   d) tap

5) alarm
   a) öryggiskerfi
   b) millifærsla
   c) að lána
   d) ferðatékki

6) to pay
   a) útgjöld
   b) banki
   c) að borga
   d) kaup

7) ATM
   a) viðskiptavinur
   b) kreditkort
   c) hraðbanki
   d) tékki

8) funds transfer
   a) millifærsla
   b) öryggisskápur
   c) sparnaður
   d) veðsetning

9) capital
   a) tap
   b) hraðbanki
   c) fjármagn
   d) öryggisvörður

10) withdrawal
   a) kaup
   b) bankayfirlit
   c) úttekt
   d) peningur

Word Quiz #47 - Bank

Choose the best Icelandic word to match the English word.

1) mortgage
 a) afrit
 b) tékki
 c) viðskiptavinur
 d) veðsetning

2) to cash
 a) sparnaðarreikningur
 b) að draga inn
 c) tap
 d) öryggisvörður

3) account
 a) úttekt
 b) fjármagn
 c) aðgangur
 d) ferðatékki

4) funds transfer
 a) prósenta
 b) klink
 c) millifærsla
 d) fjármagn

5) account balance
 a) veðsetning
 b) gjaldmiðill
 c) bankayfirlit
 d) bankastaða

6) bank statement
 a) innlögn
 b) virði
 c) bankayfirlit
 d) færslur

7) to deposit
 a) að leggja inn
 b) færslur
 c) að borga
 d) gjaldmiðlavirði

8) loss
 a) tap
 b) færslur
 c) millifærsla
 d) banki

9) fee
 a) debetkort
 b) gjald
 c) afrit
 d) öryggisskápur

10) deposit
 a) aðgangur
 b) innlögn
 c) innheimta
 d) að lána

Word Quiz #48 - Bank

Choose the best Icelandic word to match the English word.

1) to change
 a) afgangur
 b) banka reikningur
 c) að Skipta
 d) afgreiðslumaður

2) current account
 a) debetkort
 b) núverandi aðgangur
 c) að lána
 d) útgjöld

3) to deposit
 a) að leggja inn
 b) að draga inn
 c) gjaldkeri
 d) útgjöld

4) withdrawal
 a) lánstraust
 b) gjaldmiðill
 c) úttekt
 d) klink

5) receipt
 a) bankastaða
 b) afrit
 c) vextir
 d) viðskiptavinur

6) credit card
 a) yfirmaður
 b) fjármagn
 c) bankayfirlit
 d) kreditkort

7) account
 a) aðgangur
 b) útgjöld
 c) að skrifa undir
 d) að lána

8) debit card
 a) að millifæra
 b) gjald
 c) debetkort
 d) að leggja inn

9) share
 a) skuld
 b) millifærsla
 c) að lána
 d) hlutabréf

10) teller
 a) hraðbanki
 b) gjaldkeri
 c) millifærsla
 d) dollarar

Word Quiz #49 - Bank

Choose the best Icelandic word to match the English word.

1) safe
a) öryggisskápur
b) samningur
c) kaup
d) debetkort

2) currency
a) að millifæra
b) gjaldmiðill
c) vextir
d) að Skipta

3) percentage
a) hlutabréf
b) prósenta
c) lán
d) gjaldmiðlavirði

4) credit card
a) bankayfirlit
b) núverandi aðgangur
c) vextir
d) kreditkort

5) bank
a) seðill
b) yfirmaður
c) afgreiðslumaður
d) banki

6) exchange rate
a) fjármagn
b) öryggiskerfi
c) gjaldmiðlavirði
d) lán

7) interest
a) sparnaðarreikningur
b) klink
c) vextir
d) viðskiptavinur

8) bank statement
a) dollarar
b) öryggiskerfi
c) fjárhæð
d) bankayfirlit

9) loss
a) að taka út
b) lán
c) greiðsla
d) tap

10) cash
a) seðill
b) geymsla
c) tékkabók
d) öryggisvörður

Word Quiz #50 - Bank

Choose the best Icelandic word to match the English word.

1) money exchanger
 a) debetkort
 b) skuld
 c) að borga
 d) gjaldmiðlaskipti

2) capital
 a) hraðbanki
 b) fjármagn
 c) að leggja inn
 d) gróði

3) purchase
 a) núverandi aðgangur
 b) lánstraust
 c) kaup
 d) prósenta

4) payment
 a) greiðsla
 b) virði
 c) öryggisskápur
 d) hlutabréf

5) customer
 a) hlutabréf
 b) að fá lánað
 c) banka reikningur
 d) viðskiptavinur

6) loss
 a) gjaldmiðlaskipti
 b) að borga
 c) sparnaður
 d) tap

7) loan
 a) lán
 b) að borga
 c) gróði
 d) sparnaðarreikningur

8) cash
 a) geymsla
 b) peningur
 c) seðill
 d) greiðsla

9) coin
 a) klink
 b) að taka út
 c) að Skipta
 d) vextir

10) fee
 a) fjárhæð
 b) gjald
 c) gjaldmiðlavirði
 d) skuld

Word Quiz #51 - Hotel

Choose the best English word to match the Icelandic word.

1) svíta
   a) dining room
   b) suite
   c) room
   d) taxi

2) hotel
   a) garage
   b) chair
   c) bill
   d) hotel

3) útsýni
   a) maid
   b) balcony
   c) bellboy
   d) view

4) herbergisþjónusta
   a) key
   b) room service
   c) living room
   d) internet

5) stofa
   a) breakfast
   b) complaint
   c) living room
   d) price

6) stigar
   a) key
   b) receptionist
   c) staircase
   d) reception desk

7) sundlaug
   a) chair
   b) breakfast
   c) ice
   d) swimming pool

8) skilaboð
   a) breakfast
   b) loo
   c) message
   d) receptionist

9) endurgerð
   a) bellboy
   b) floor
   c) recreation
   d) air conditioning

10) bókun
   a) ground floor
   b) receptionist
   c) booking
   d) carpet

Word Quiz #52 - Hotel

Choose the best English word to match the Icelandic word.

1) teppi
  a) ground floor
  b) carpet
  c) garage
  d) receptionist

2) gestamóttaka
  a) entrance
  b) swimming pool
  c) reception desk
  d) loo

3) internet
  a) internet
  b) pillow
  c) blanket
  d) maid

4) jarðhæð
  a) doorman
  b) ground floor
  c) suite
  d) recreation

5) kvörtun
  a) suite
  b) bellboy
  c) key
  d) complaint

6) herbergi
  a) reception desk
  b) room
  c) bellboy
  d) internet

7) lyfta
  a) bill
  b) breakfast
  c) lift
  d) ice

8) stigar
  a) bill
  b) key
  c) staircase
  d) lobby

9) rúm
  a) lift
  b) entrance
  c) bed
  d) bellboy

10) verð
  a) blanket
  b) hotel
  c) price
  d) room service

Word Quiz #53 - Hotel
Choose the best English word to match the Icelandic word.

1) svíta
a) room
b) lobby
c) carpet
d) suite

2) bókun
a) booking
b) living room
c) internet
d) carpet

3) stigar
a) staircase
b) reception desk
c) ground floor
d) blanket

4) hotel
a) bed
b) doorman
c) blanket
d) hotel

5) móttaka
a) pillow
b) lobby
c) living room
d) message

6) reikningur
a) dining room
b) bill
c) receptionist
d) lift

7) ís
a) room service
b) ice
c) recreation
d) internet

8) internet
a) table
b) balcony
c) internet
d) price

9) dyravörður
a) key
b) air conditioning
c) doorman
d) loo

10) loftræsting
a) room service
b) table
c) room
d) air conditioning

Word Quiz #54 - Hotel

Choose the best English word to match the Icelandic word.

1) stóll
  a) chair
  b) bill
  c) lobby
  d) receptionist

2) morgunmatur
  a) breakfast
  b) price
  c) chair
  d) ground floor

3) reikningur
  a) view
  b) ground floor
  c) bill
  d) pillow

4) ís
  a) booking
  b) ice
  c) room
  d) key

5) kvörtun
  a) recreation
  b) doorman
  c) receptionist
  d) complaint

6) skilaboð
  a) recreation
  b) room service
  c) garage
  d) message

7) koddi
  a) ice
  b) pillow
  c) entrance
  d) view

8) herbergisþjónusta
  a) internet
  b) ground floor
  c) living room
  d) room service

9) teppi
  a) blanket
  b) doorman
  c) recreation
  d) air conditioning

10) móttaka
  a) breakfast
  b) price
  c) balcony
  d) lobby

Word Quiz #55 - Hotel

Choose the best English word to match the Icelandic word.

1) móttaka
a) view
b) balcony
c) maid
d) lobby

2) verð
a) message
b) price
c) booking
d) carpet

3) útsýni
a) floor
b) balcony
c) bed
d) view

4) stigar
a) stairs
b) dining room
c) room service
d) reception desk

5) teppi
a) hotel
b) carpet
c) key
d) swimming pool

6) matsalur
a) chair
b) ice
c) dining room
d) living room

7) kvörtun
a) suite
b) air conditioning
c) bill
d) complaint

8) dyravörður
a) chair
b) pillow
c) entrance
d) doorman

9) klósett
a) air conditioning
b) living room
c) staircase
d) loo

10) bílskúr
a) price
b) receptionist
c) stairs
d) garage

Word Quiz #56 - Hotel

Choose the best English word to match the Icelandic word.

1) hotel
a) maid
b) swimming pool
c) staircase
d) hotel

2) lyfta
a) ice
b) staircase
c) lift
d) complaint

3) stigar
a) bill
b) floor
c) stairs
d) lift

4) svíta
a) table
b) ice
c) room
d) suite

5) bílskúr
a) room service
b) swimming pool
c) bellboy
d) garage

6) teppi
a) reception desk
b) recreation
c) swimming pool
d) blanket

7) matsalur
a) dining room
b) booking
c) complaint
d) doorman

8) rúm
a) pillow
b) breakfast
c) bed
d) price

9) móttaka
a) lobby
b) taxi
c) lift
d) loo

10) inngangur
a) ground floor
b) taxi
c) lift
d) entrance

Word Quiz #57 - Hotel

Choose the best English word to match the Icelandic word.

1) lyfta
 a) taxi
 b) lift
 c) stairs
 d) dining room

2) endurgerð
 a) recreation
 b) stairs
 c) booking
 d) hotel

3) internet
 a) maid
 b) internet
 c) hotel
 d) chair

4) gestamóttaka
 a) lobby
 b) balcony
 c) reception desk
 d) bellboy

5) útsýni
 a) swimming pool
 b) view
 c) checkout
 d) bed

6) bílskúr
 a) message
 b) key
 c) garage
 d) loo

7) sundlaug
 a) staircase
 b) loo
 c) living room
 d) swimming pool

8) hotel
 a) bellboy
 b) hotel
 c) table
 d) staircase

9) hæð
 a) hotel
 b) floor
 c) view
 d) receptionist

10) afgreiðsla
 a) ice
 b) suite
 c) air conditioning
 d) checkout

Word Quiz #58 - Hotel

Choose the best English word to match the Icelandic word.

1) rúm
 a) staircase
 b) reception desk
 c) maid
 d) bed

2) stigar
 a) stairs
 b) table
 c) carpet
 d) receptionist

3) gestamóttaka
 a) internet
 b) blanket
 c) loo
 d) reception desk

4) leigubíll
 a) booking
 b) lift
 c) receptionist
 d) taxi

5) gestamóttakandi
 a) blanket
 b) receptionist
 c) staircase
 d) lobby

6) jarðhæð
 a) chair
 b) key
 c) booking
 d) ground floor

7) endurgerð
 a) recreation
 b) floor
 c) balcony
 d) floor

8) reikningur
 a) bill
 b) pillow
 c) recreation
 d) lift

9) móttaka
 a) breakfast
 b) entrance
 c) view
 d) lobby

10) vikapiltur
 a) bellboy
 b) swimming pool
 c) pillow
 d) lobby

Word Quiz #59 - Hotel

Choose the best English word to match the Icelandic word.

1) útsýni
  a) view
  b) taxi
  c) table
  d) room

2) stóll
  a) chair
  b) complaint
  c) room service
  d) taxi

3) ís
  a) booking
  b) air conditioning
  c) ice
  d) bed

4) rúm
  a) checkout
  b) stairs
  c) bed
  d) reception desk

5) koddi
  a) pillow
  b) balcony
  c) carpet
  d) breakfast

6) verð
  a) blanket
  b) floor
  c) price
  d) loo

7) klósett
  a) loo
  b) taxi
  c) checkout
  d) entrance

8) bílskúr
  a) swimming pool
  b) receptionist
  c) chair
  d) garage

9) teppi
  a) ice
  b) blanket
  c) breakfast
  d) internet

10) stigar
  a) room
  b) stairs
  c) room service
  d) air conditioning

Word Quiz #60 - Hotel

Choose the best English word to match the Icelandic word.

1) herbergisþjónusta
   a) recreation
   b) room service
   c) dining room
   d) checkout

2) rúm
   a) garage
   b) bed
   c) floor
   d) key

3) lykill
   a) key
   b) receptionist
   c) bellboy
   d) checkout

4) borð
   a) table
   b) ground floor
   c) breakfast
   d) room

5) skilaboð
   a) stairs
   b) ice
   c) message
   d) bill

6) internet
   a) garage
   b) key
   c) bill
   d) internet

7) gestamóttakandi
   a) pillow
   b) receptionist
   c) room
   d) bellboy

8) stigar
   a) balcony
   b) staircase
   c) loo
   d) suite

9) dyravörður
   a) receptionist
   b) table
   c) breakfast
   d) doorman

10) stóll
   a) staircase
   b) chair
   c) doorman
   d) pillow

Word Quiz #61 - Hotel

Choose the best English word to match the Icelandic word.

1) teppi
 a) carpet
 b) lobby
 c) suite
 d) balcony

2) koddi
 a) pillow
 b) key
 c) checkout
 d) entrance

3) skilaboð
 a) swimming pool
 b) hotel
 c) message
 d) balcony

4) stigar
 a) taxi
 b) living room
 c) suite
 d) stairs

5) svíta
 a) price
 b) suite
 c) stairs
 d) loo

6) útsýni
 a) bill
 b) bellboy
 c) view
 d) swimming pool

7) morgunmatur
 a) breakfast
 b) blanket
 c) internet
 d) message

8) herbergisþjónusta
 a) price
 b) entrance
 c) room service
 d) bed

9) stigar
 a) staircase
 b) suite
 c) breakfast
 d) swimming pool

10) hotel
 a) hotel
 b) lobby
 c) swimming pool
 d) recreation

Word Quiz #62 - Hotel

Choose the best English word to match the Icelandic word.

1) leigubíll
  a) bill
  b) ground floor
  c) booking
  d) taxi

2) morgunmatur
  a) breakfast
  b) bellboy
  c) bed
  d) bill

3) inngangur
  a) complaint
  b) entrance
  c) pillow
  d) dining room

4) verð
  a) air conditioning
  b) stairs
  c) price
  d) recreation

5) kvörtun
  a) complaint
  b) garage
  c) view
  d) message

6) klósett
  a) lobby
  b) loo
  c) blanket
  d) checkout

7) rúm
  a) bill
  b) bed
  c) checkout
  d) carpet

8) lykill
  a) key
  b) garage
  c) maid
  d) internet

9) hotel
  a) swimming pool
  b) hotel
  c) view
  d) price

10) dyravörður
  a) key
  b) swimming pool
  c) doorman
  d) lift

Word Quiz #63 - Hotel

Choose the best English word to match the Icelandic word.

1) endurgerð
a) internet
b) recreation
c) ground floor
d) maid

2) dyravörður
a) doorman
b) loo
c) key
d) receptionist

3) afgreiðsla
a) room
b) receptionist
c) checkout
d) key

4) svíta
a) room
b) suite
c) blanket
d) bill

5) bílskúr
a) garage
b) lobby
c) bellboy
d) dining room

6) stigar
a) dining room
b) chair
c) staircase
d) recreation

7) loftræsting
a) air conditioning
b) bed
c) blanket
d) reception desk

8) lykill
a) ground floor
b) complaint
c) room service
d) key

9) bókun
a) garage
b) dining room
c) staircase
d) booking

10) koddi
a) price
b) key
c) complaint
d) pillow

Word Quiz #64 - Hotel

Choose the best Icelandic word to match the English word.

1) price
a) verð
b) hotel
c) dyravörður
d) skilaboð

2) ground floor
a) hæð
b) koddi
c) stofa
d) jarðhæð

3) recreation
a) endurgerð
b) afgreiðsla
c) loftræsting
d) matsalur

4) living room
a) dyravörður
b) rúm
c) kvörtun
d) stofa

5) stairs
a) loftræsting
b) stigar
c) móttaka
d) endurgerð

6) view
a) koddi
b) útsýni
c) borð
d) stofa

7) complaint
a) endurgerð
b) stofa
c) afgreiðsla
d) kvörtun

8) reception desk
a) morgunmatur
b) útsýni
c) gestamóttaka
d) bókun

9) bill
a) herbergi
b) internet
c) vikapiltur
d) reikningur

10) bellboy
a) loftræsting
b) skilaboð
c) vikapiltur
d) móttaka

Word Quiz #65 - Hotel

Choose the best Icelandic word to match the English word.

1) chair
   a) stóll
   b) hotel
   c) stigar
   d) hæð

2) price
   a) borð
   b) verð
   c) þerna
   d) reikningur

3) bed
   a) ís
   b) stofa
   c) rúm
   d) endurgerð

4) staircase
   a) hotel
   b) stigar
   c) bílskúr
   d) inngangur

5) ground floor
   a) lyfta
   b) jarðhæð
   c) borð
   d) koddi

6) lobby
   a) rúm
   b) leigubíll
   c) móttaka
   d) endurgerð

7) room service
   a) herbergisþjónusta
   b) svíta
   c) skilaboð
   d) stóll

8) floor
   a) hæð
   b) útsýni
   c) jarðhæð
   d) teppi

9) dining room
   a) bílskúr
   b) dyravörður
   c) matsalur
   d) teppi

10) hotel
   a) hotel
   b) jarðhæð
   c) sundlaug
   d) stóll

Word Quiz #66 - Hotel

Choose the best Icelandic word to match the English word.

1) price
a) verð
b) herbergisþjónusta
c) hotel
d) stigar

2) recreation
a) endurgerð
b) vikapiltur
c) internet
d) rúm

3) maid
a) internet
b) þerna
c) svalir
d) morgunmatur

4) floor
a) kvörtun
b) ís
c) útsýni
d) hæð

5) entrance
a) gestamóttaka
b) stigar
c) inngangur
d) kvörtun

6) doorman
a) gestamóttaka
b) rúm
c) teppi
d) dyravörður

7) lift
a) rúm
b) móttaka
c) verð
d) lyfta

8) bellboy
a) þerna
b) lykill
c) svíta
d) vikapiltur

9) blanket
a) bílskúr
b) lyfta
c) stigar
d) teppi

10) view
a) stofa
b) útsýni
c) hæð
d) móttaka

Word Quiz #67 - Hotel

Choose the best Icelandic word to match the English word.

1) room
  a) gestamóttakandi
  b) matsalur
  c) stigar
  d) herbergi

2) reception desk
  a) gestamóttaka
  b) svíta
  c) stigar
  d) teppi

3) swimming pool
  a) hotel
  b) reikningur
  c) stóll
  d) sundlaug

4) balcony
  a) hotel
  b) morgunmatur
  c) svalir
  d) stóll

5) taxi
  a) leigubíll
  b) dyravörður
  c) internet
  d) ís

6) air conditioning
  a) dyravörður
  b) ís
  c) loftræsting
  d) útsýni

7) checkout
  a) stóll
  b) afgreiðsla
  c) matsalur
  d) leigubíll

8) view
  a) útsýni
  b) stofa
  c) afgreiðsla
  d) klósett

9) ice
  a) hæð
  b) matsalur
  c) rúm
  d) ís

10) bill
  a) lykill
  b) reikningur
  c) herbergisþjónusta
  d) leigubíll

Word Quiz #68 - Hotel

Choose the best Icelandic word to match the English word.

1) lift
   a) bókun
   b) rúm
   c) loftræsting
   d) lyfta

2) living room
   a) leigubíll
   b) lyfta
   c) stofa
   d) teppi

3) lobby
   a) gestamóttakandi
   b) inngangur
   c) skilaboð
   d) móttaka

4) ice
   a) endurgerð
   b) ís
   c) hotel
   d) móttaka

5) key
   a) lykill
   b) stofa
   c) vikapiltur
   d) svalir

6) internet
   a) hotel
   b) skilaboð
   c) koddi
   d) internet

7) maid
   a) endurgerð
   b) ís
   c) lykill
   d) þerna

8) price
   a) internet
   b) matsalur
   c) verð
   d) skilaboð

9) suite
   a) vikapiltur
   b) koddi
   c) svíta
   d) stigar

10) bellboy
   a) koddi
   b) vikapiltur
   c) gestamóttaka
   d) herbergi

Word Quiz #69 - Hotel

Choose the best Icelandic word to match the English word.

1) doorman
 a) útsýni
 b) matsalur
 c) dyravörður
 d) herbergisþjónusta

2) bellboy
 a) borð
 b) þerna
 c) vikapiltur
 d) reikningur

3) table
 a) borð
 b) stofa
 c) leigubíll
 d) stigar

4) key
 a) kvörtun
 b) lykill
 c) sundlaug
 d) jarðhæð

5) price
 a) verð
 b) svalir
 c) stigar
 d) herbergi

6) garage
 a) bílskúr
 b) morgunmatur
 c) koddi
 d) bókun

7) message
 a) herbergi
 b) bílskúr
 c) útsýni
 d) skilaboð

8) swimming pool
 a) bókun
 b) inngangur
 c) sundlaug
 d) internet

9) reception desk
 a) bókun
 b) borð
 c) útsýni
 d) gestamóttaka

10) staircase
 a) herbergisþjónusta
 b) koddi
 c) stigar
 d) stóll

Word Quiz #70 - Hotel

Choose the best Icelandic word to match the English word.

1) garage
a) bílskúr
b) útsýni
c) gestamóttakandi
d) lyfta

2) suite
a) svíta
b) skilaboð
c) stóll
d) teppi

3) hotel
a) svíta
b) hotel
c) loftræsting
d) bókun

4) lobby
a) lyfta
b) herbergisþjónusta
c) hæð
d) móttaka

5) air conditioning
a) þerna
b) bókun
c) loftræsting
d) herbergisþjónusta

6) dining room
a) matsalur
b) leigubíll
c) teppi
d) stóll

7) receptionist
a) hæð
b) verð
c) gestamóttakandi
d) endurgerð

8) recreation
a) endurgerð
b) móttaka
c) hotel
d) svíta

9) internet
a) gestamóttakandi
b) internet
c) hotel
d) loftræsting

10) pillow
a) jarðhæð
b) svíta
c) lykill
d) koddi

Word Quiz #71 - Hotel

Choose the best Icelandic word to match the English word.

1) price
   a) móttaka
   b) verð
   c) lykill
   d) stigar

2) maid
   a) herbergi
   b) bílskúr
   c) matsalur
   d) þerna

3) staircase
   a) stigar
   b) klósett
   c) útsýni
   d) gestamóttakandi

4) living room
   a) stóll
   b) stofa
   c) útsýni
   d) verð

5) stairs
   a) stigar
   b) svíta
   c) skilaboð
   d) borð

6) booking
   a) bókun
   b) klósett
   c) inngangur
   d) útsýni

7) blanket
   a) hæð
   b) herbergisþjónusta
   c) teppi
   d) koddi

8) doorman
   a) gestamóttaka
   b) jarðhæð
   c) skilaboð
   d) dyravörður

9) room
   a) herbergi
   b) svíta
   c) svalir
   d) þerna

10) message
   a) leigubíll
   b) jarðhæð
   c) teppi
   d) skilaboð

Word Quiz #72 - Hotel

Choose the best Icelandic word to match the English word.

1) bed
 a) gestamóttaka
 b) rúm
 c) leigubíll
 d) hæð

2) table
 a) endurgerð
 b) teppi
 c) bókun
 d) borð

3) carpet
 a) rúm
 b) koddi
 c) teppi
 d) internet

4) internet
 a) jarðhæð
 b) móttaka
 c) internet
 d) herbergi

5) living room
 a) hotel
 b) kvörtun
 c) svíta
 d) stofa

6) floor
 a) teppi
 b) hæð
 c) hotel
 d) gestamóttaka

7) reception desk
 a) gestamóttaka
 b) þerna
 c) stofa
 d) bílskúr

8) view
 a) hotel
 b) útsýni
 c) svalir
 d) loftræsting

9) price
 a) inngangur
 b) rúm
 c) móttaka
 d) verð

10) garage
 a) bílskúr
 b) afgreiðsla
 c) herbergisþjónusta
 d) stigar

Word Quiz #73 - Hotel

Choose the best Icelandic word to match the English word.

1) bill
 a) jarðhæð
 b) rúm
 c) reikningur
 d) móttaka

2) swimming pool
 a) borð
 b) reikningur
 c) sundlaug
 d) stofa

3) chair
 a) stóll
 b) koddi
 c) stofa
 d) gestamóttaka

4) price
 a) verð
 b) lykill
 c) morgunmatur
 d) borð

5) room
 a) herbergi
 b) rúm
 c) stóll
 d) útsýni

6) ground floor
 a) jarðhæð
 b) útsýni
 c) morgunmatur
 d) teppi

7) suite
 a) vikapiltur
 b) sundlaug
 c) hotel
 d) svíta

8) lobby
 a) lykill
 b) dyravörður
 c) móttaka
 d) skilaboð

9) stairs
 a) svalir
 b) stigar
 c) inngangur
 d) svíta

10) taxi
 a) verð
 b) leigubíll
 c) borð
 d) rúm

Word Quiz #74 - Hotel

Choose the best Icelandic word to match the English word.

1) stairs
  a) herbergi
  b) hæð
  c) hotel
  d) stigar

2) table
  a) útsýni
  b) dyravörður
  c) borð
  d) reikningur

3) breakfast
  a) matsalur
  b) internet
  c) morgunmatur
  d) hæð

4) taxi
  a) afgreiðsla
  b) leigubíll
  c) lykill
  d) sundlaug

5) view
  a) útsýni
  b) teppi
  c) gestamóttakandi
  d) þerna

6) blanket
  a) teppi
  b) þerna
  c) hæð
  d) stigar

7) receptionist
  a) skilaboð
  b) hotel
  c) gestamóttakandi
  d) teppi

8) air conditioning
  a) koddi
  b) klósett
  c) loftræsting
  d) gestamóttaka

9) bill
  a) reikningur
  b) morgunmatur
  c) leigubíll
  d) hæð

10) chair
  a) borð
  b) svíta
  c) hæð
  d) stóll

Word Quiz #75 - Hotel

Choose the best Icelandic word to match the English word.

1) swimming pool
  a) lyfta
  b) teppi
  c) herbergi
  d) sundlaug

2) reception desk
  a) endurgerð
  b) stóll
  c) gestamóttaka
  d) dyravörður

3) booking
  a) leigubíll
  b) skilaboð
  c) bókun
  d) þerna

4) garage
  a) klósett
  b) bílskúr
  c) vikapiltur
  d) stóll

5) air conditioning
  a) morgunmatur
  b) ís
  c) hotel
  d) loftræsting

6) maid
  a) rúm
  b) endurgerð
  c) þerna
  d) kvörtun

7) bed
  a) rúm
  b) afgreiðsla
  c) stofa
  d) útsýni

8) bellboy
  a) rúm
  b) sundlaug
  c) vikapiltur
  d) teppi

9) table
  a) stigar
  b) kvörtun
  c) borð
  d) leigubíll

10) checkout
  a) vikapiltur
  b) ís
  c) klósett
  d) afgreiðsla

Word Quiz #76 - Pharmacy
Choose the best English word to match the Icelandic word.

1) plástur
a) bandage
b) prescription
c) penicillin
d) pill

2) innspýting
a) antibiotic
b) dental floss
c) injection
d) prescription

3) tafla
a) aspirin
b) cortisone
c) pharmacy
d) pill

4) sýróp
a) laxative
b) syrup
c) prescription
d) pharmacist

5) sýklalyf
a) medicine
b) prescription
c) antibiotic
d) pill

6) apótek
a) medicine
b) pharmacy
c) insulin
d) antibiotic

7) hitamælir
a) medicine
b) thermometer
c) cortisone
d) insulin

8) vítamín
a) iodine
b) syrup
c) ointment
d) vitamin

9) lyfseðill
a) prescription
b) cortisone
c) aspirin
d) vitamin

10) áburður
a) tablet
b) pill
c) ointment
d) iodine

Word Quiz #77 - Pharmacy
Choose the best English word to match the Icelandic word.

1) vítamín
  a) vitamin
  b) iodine
  c) tablet
  d) pill

2) sýklalyf
  a) iodine
  b) bandage
  c) tablet
  d) antibiotic

3) tafla
  a) insulin
  b) prescription
  c) pill
  d) bandage

4) plástur
  a) laxative
  b) pill
  c) iodine
  d) bandage

5) innspýting
  a) cortisone
  b) thermometer
  c) pharmacy
  d) injection

6) lyf
  a) bandage
  b) medicine
  c) dental floss
  d) syrup

7) læknir
  a) dental floss
  b) pharmacist
  c) cortisone
  d) pill

8) kortisón
  a) cortisone
  b) injection
  c) syrup
  d) bandage

9) hægðalyf
  a) ointment
  b) medicine
  c) laxative
  d) antibiotic

10) hitamælir
  a) thermometer
  b) tablet
  c) pharmacist
  d) aspirin

Word Quiz #78 - Pharmacy

Choose the best English word to match the Icelandic word.

1) joð
   a) pharmacy
   b) antibiotic
   c) pharmacist
   d) iodine

2) sýklalyf
   a) pill
   b) antibiotic
   c) injection
   d) dental floss

3) hitamælir
   a) ointment
   b) aspirin
   c) insulin
   d) thermometer

4) vítamín
   a) pharmacy
   b) thermometer
   c) vitamin
   d) aspirin

5) apótek
   a) antibiotic
   b) cortisone
   c) injection
   d) pharmacy

6) innspýting
   a) prescription
   b) bandage
   c) dental floss
   d) injection

7) lyfseðill
   a) aspirin
   b) pharmacy
   c) prescription
   d) medicine

8) munnskol
   a) injection
   b) ointment
   c) tablet
   d) dental floss

9) insulin
   a) prescription
   b) bandage
   c) insulin
   d) pharmacy

10) plástur
   a) tablet
   b) laxative
   c) cortisone
   d) bandage

Word Quiz #79 - Pharmacy

Choose the best English word to match the Icelandic word.

1) joð
a) syrup
b) pill
c) antibiotic
d) iodine

2) læknir
a) laxative
b) syrup
c) pill
d) pharmacist

3) hægðalyf
a) penicillin
b) pharmacist
c) aspirin
d) laxative

4) lyfseðill
a) laxative
b) pill
c) prescription
d) bandage

5) kortisón
a) injection
b) insulin
c) cortisone
d) tablet

6) pensilín
a) dental floss
b) penicillin
c) laxative
d) aspirin

7) munnskol
a) dental floss
b) aspirin
c) thermometer
d) prescription

8) vítamín
a) vitamin
b) insulin
c) laxative
d) prescription

9) insulin
a) insulin
b) injection
c) prescription
d) iodine

10) lyf
a) dental floss
b) injection
c) insulin
d) medicine

Word Quiz #80 - Pharmacy

Choose the best English word to match the Icelandic word.

1) aspirin
 a) injection
 b) penicillin
 c) pill
 d) aspirin

2) hægðalyf
 a) penicillin
 b) vitamin
 c) bandage
 d) laxative

3) sýróp
 a) pharmacist
 b) syrup
 c) ointment
 d) pill

4) tafla
 a) tablet
 b) ointment
 c) medicine
 d) thermometer

5) insulin
 a) aspirin
 b) vitamin
 c) insulin
 d) bandage

6) vítamín
 a) syrup
 b) prescription
 c) pill
 d) vitamin

7) lyfseðill
 a) pharmacist
 b) prescription
 c) ointment
 d) pharmacy

8) pensilín
 a) vitamin
 b) insulin
 c) penicillin
 d) aspirin

9) innspýting
 a) aspirin
 b) injection
 c) syrup
 d) laxative

10) apótek
 a) pharmacist
 b) injection
 c) pharmacy
 d) tablet

Word Quiz #81 - Pharmacy

Choose the best English word to match the Icelandic word.

1) lyf
a) vitamin
b) tablet
c) medicine
d) laxative

2) plástur
a) tablet
b) pharmacy
c) insulin
d) bandage

3) innspýting
a) pill
b) penicillin
c) injection
d) aspirin

4) hægðalyf
a) iodine
b) prescription
c) aspirin
d) laxative

5) læknir
a) pharmacist
b) bandage
c) vitamin
d) prescription

6) lyfseðill
a) medicine
b) prescription
c) pharmacist
d) syrup

7) aspirin
a) aspirin
b) insulin
c) thermometer
d) vitamin

8) vítamín
a) vitamin
b) aspirin
c) pharmacist
d) thermometer

9) pensilín
a) penicillin
b) dental floss
c) antibiotic
d) tablet

10) áburður
a) ointment
b) laxative
c) penicillin
d) medicine

Word Quiz #82 - Pharmacy

Choose the best English word to match the Icelandic word.

1) joð
   a) medicine
   b) laxative
   c) iodine
   d) pharmacist

2) hægðalyf
   a) laxative
   b) thermometer
   c) cortisone
   d) vitamin

3) hitamælir
   a) aspirin
   b) laxative
   c) thermometer
   d) dental floss

4) lyf
   a) laxative
   b) medicine
   c) dental floss
   d) cortisone

5) tafla
   a) dental floss
   b) iodine
   c) bandage
   d) pill

6) sýróp
   a) pharmacy
   b) syrup
   c) injection
   d) penicillin

7) lyfseðill
   a) ointment
   b) tablet
   c) laxative
   d) prescription

8) insulin
   a) ointment
   b) insulin
   c) cortisone
   d) penicillin

9) sýklalyf
   a) antibiotic
   b) vitamin
   c) penicillin
   d) syrup

10) læknir
   a) aspirin
   b) bandage
   c) pharmacist
   d) injection

Word Quiz #83 - Pharmacy

Choose the best English word to match the Icelandic word.

1) apótek
a) pharmacy
b) penicillin
c) thermometer
d) laxative

2) tafla
a) pharmacist
b) aspirin
c) insulin
d) tablet

3) lyf
a) penicillin
b) cortisone
c) medicine
d) dental floss

4) vítamín
a) ointment
b) dental floss
c) syrup
d) vitamin

5) aspirin
a) pharmacist
b) aspirin
c) antibiotic
d) bandage

6) sýróp
a) laxative
b) bandage
c) syrup
d) aspirin

7) hitamælir
a) pill
b) thermometer
c) pharmacy
d) tablet

8) kortisón
a) laxative
b) cortisone
c) syrup
d) bandage

9) joð
a) iodine
b) injection
c) tablet
d) medicine

10) hægðalyf
a) prescription
b) laxative
c) tablet
d) penicillin

Word Quiz #84 - Pharmacy

Choose the best English word to match the Icelandic word.

1) pensilín
 a) prescription
 b) penicillin
 c) laxative
 d) vitamin

2) læknir
 a) pharmacist
 b) ointment
 c) prescription
 d) vitamin

3) plástur
 a) bandage
 b) vitamin
 c) laxative
 d) medicine

4) tafla
 a) pharmacy
 b) aspirin
 c) tablet
 d) insulin

5) sýróp
 a) aspirin
 b) tablet
 c) syrup
 d) antibiotic

6) aspirin
 a) aspirin
 b) cortisone
 c) bandage
 d) insulin

7) apótek
 a) syrup
 b) prescription
 c) aspirin
 d) pharmacy

8) áburður
 a) syrup
 b) ointment
 c) injection
 d) bandage

9) lyf
 a) medicine
 b) cortisone
 c) pharmacist
 d) pharmacy

10) innspýting
 a) thermometer
 b) injection
 c) antibiotic
 d) tablet

Word Quiz #85 - Pharmacy

Choose the best English word to match the Icelandic word.

1) plástur
  a) pill
  b) injection
  c) medicine
  d) bandage

2) vítamín
  a) thermometer
  b) pharmacist
  c) vitamin
  d) aspirin

3) joð
  a) pharmacy
  b) thermometer
  c) iodine
  d) antibiotic

4) tafla
  a) penicillin
  b) thermometer
  c) vitamin
  d) pill

5) lyfseðill
  a) vitamin
  b) thermometer
  c) pill
  d) prescription

6) apótek
  a) pill
  b) bandage
  c) cortisone
  d) pharmacy

7) áburður
  a) iodine
  b) injection
  c) medicine
  d) ointment

8) hitamælir
  a) penicillin
  b) antibiotic
  c) vitamin
  d) thermometer

9) insulin
  a) injection
  b) pill
  c) bandage
  d) insulin

10) sýróp
  a) dental floss
  b) medicine
  c) syrup
  d) thermometer

Word Quiz #86 - Pharmacy
Choose the best English word to match the Icelandic word.

1) tafla
  a) tablet
  b) injection
  c) pill
  d) aspirin

2) kortisón
  a) tablet
  b) vitamin
  c) pill
  d) cortisone

3) áburður
  a) bandage
  b) vitamin
  c) syrup
  d) ointment

4) tafla
  a) penicillin
  b) vitamin
  c) tablet
  d) thermometer

5) hægðalyf
  a) prescription
  b) iodine
  c) laxative
  d) pharmacist

6) aspirin
  a) penicillin
  b) ointment
  c) medicine
  d) aspirin

7) innspýting
  a) prescription
  b) injection
  c) medicine
  d) ointment

8) joð
  a) iodine
  b) pill
  c) insulin
  d) penicillin

9) munnskol
  a) pharmacist
  b) ointment
  c) dental floss
  d) insulin

10) vítamín
  a) tablet
  b) antibiotic
  c) laxative
  d) vitamin

Word Quiz #87 - Pharmacy

Choose the best English word to match the Icelandic word.

1) munnskol
  a) tablet
  b) dental floss
  c) laxative
  d) thermometer

2) sýklalyf
  a) pharmacist
  b) antibiotic
  c) medicine
  d) pharmacy

3) tafla
  a) pill
  b) pharmacy
  c) aspirin
  d) iodine

4) lyfseðill
  a) iodine
  b) prescription
  c) pharmacist
  d) pill

5) joð
  a) bandage
  b) iodine
  c) laxative
  d) pill

6) pensilín
  a) medicine
  b) penicillin
  c) pharmacy
  d) ointment

7) kortisón
  a) cortisone
  b) pharmacy
  c) pill
  d) antibiotic

8) vítamín
  a) syrup
  b) insulin
  c) vitamin
  d) injection

9) læknir
  a) pharmacist
  b) thermometer
  c) bandage
  d) injection

10) sýróp
  a) pill
  b) vitamin
  c) pharmacist
  d) syrup

Word Quiz #88 - Pharmacy

Choose the best English word to match the Icelandic word.

1) áburður
   a) insulin
   b) iodine
   c) tablet
   d) ointment

2) pensilín
   a) tablet
   b) thermometer
   c) aspirin
   d) penicillin

3) insulin
   a) tablet
   b) insulin
   c) iodine
   d) pharmacist

4) joð
   a) pharmacy
   b) penicillin
   c) pill
   d) iodine

5) tafla
   a) ointment
   b) tablet
   c) pill
   d) vitamin

6) lyfseðill
   a) syrup
   b) prescription
   c) ointment
   d) antibiotic

7) vítamín
   a) vitamin
   b) prescription
   c) cortisone
   d) pharmacist

8) plástur
   a) penicillin
   b) dental floss
   c) bandage
   d) ointment

9) apótek
   a) tablet
   b) pharmacy
   c) penicillin
   d) thermometer

10) innspýting
   a) cortisone
   b) injection
   c) dental floss
   d) ointment

Word Quiz #89 - Pharmacy

Choose the best Icelandic word to match the English word.

1) dental floss
 a) munnskol
 b) læknir
 c) kortisón
 d) pensilín

2) antibiotic
 a) plástur
 b) innspýting
 c) sýklalyf
 d) kortisón

3) laxative
 a) hitamælir
 b) joð
 c) hægðalyf
 d) aspirin

4) cortisone
 a) insulin
 b) kortisón
 c) hitamælir
 d) munnskol

5) syrup
 a) sýklalyf
 b) pensilín
 c) joð
 d) sýróp

6) pharmacist
 a) hægðalyf
 b) innspýting
 c) pensilín
 d) læknir

7) insulin
 a) sýróp
 b) insulin
 c) lyf
 d) vítamín

8) pill
 a) apótek
 b) joð
 c) tafla
 d) munnskol

9) tablet
 a) hitamælir
 b) tafla
 c) aspirin
 d) plástur

10) aspirin
 a) plástur
 b) læknir
 c) aspirin
 d) apótek

Word Quiz #90 - Pharmacy

Choose the best Icelandic word to match the English word.

1) cortisone
   a) munnskol
   b) lyf
   c) áburður
   d) kortisón

2) pharmacy
   a) innspýting
   b) apótek
   c) aspirin
   d) plástur

3) laxative
   a) hægðalyf
   b) hitamælir
   c) lyf
   d) joð

4) tablet
   a) læknir
   b) pensilín
   c) insulin
   d) tafla

5) dental floss
   a) tafla
   b) lyf
   c) munnskol
   d) hitamælir

6) antibiotic
   a) munnskol
   b) áburður
   c) sýklalyf
   d) tafla

7) pill
   a) vítamín
   b) tafla
   c) joð
   d) sýklalyf

8) bandage
   a) joð
   b) plástur
   c) tafla
   d) kortisón

9) ointment
   a) pensilín
   b) tafla
   c) áburður
   d) insulin

10) prescription
   a) insulin
   b) joð
   c) hægðalyf
   d) lyfseðill

Word Quiz #91 - Pharmacy

Choose the best Icelandic word to match the English word.

1) ointment
 a) læknir
 b) hitamælir
 c) joð
 d) áburður

2) cortisone
 a) áburður
 b) plástur
 c) lyf
 d) kortisón

3) iodine
 a) joð
 b) læknir
 c) munnskol
 d) lyfseðill

4) vitamin
 a) plástur
 b) sýróp
 c) vítamín
 d) aspirin

5) insulin
 a) hitamælir
 b) sýróp
 c) insulin
 d) innspýting

6) laxative
 a) áburður
 b) sýróp
 c) læknir
 d) hægðalyf

7) antibiotic
 a) sýklalyf
 b) sýróp
 c) læknir
 d) joð

8) bandage
 a) sýklalyf
 b) lyf
 c) plástur
 d) hægðalyf

9) prescription
 a) lyfseðill
 b) tafla
 c) hitamælir
 d) innspýting

10) thermometer
 a) lyf
 b) hitamælir
 c) áburður
 d) plástur

Word Quiz #92 - Pharmacy

Choose the best Icelandic word to match the English word.

1) prescription
a) innspýting
b) joð
c) lyfseðill
d) tafla

2) pharmacist
a) læknir
b) tafla
c) lyf
d) hitamælir

3) penicillin
a) pensilín
b) innspýting
c) plástur
d) insulin

4) cortisone
a) sýklalyf
b) kortisón
c) hitamælir
d) innspýting

5) insulin
a) tafla
b) hitamælir
c) insulin
d) apótek

6) bandage
a) vítamín
b) tafla
c) plástur
d) aspirin

7) thermometer
a) innspýting
b) sýklalyf
c) hitamælir
d) vítamín

8) injection
a) innspýting
b) pensilín
c) tafla
d) plástur

9) pharmacy
a) apótek
b) aspirin
c) læknir
d) sýróp

10) ointment
a) plástur
b) lyf
c) joð
d) áburður

Word Quiz #93 - Pharmacy

Choose the best Icelandic word to match the English word.

1) pharmacy
   a) pensilín
   b) kortisón
   c) lyf
   d) apótek

2) thermometer
   a) hitamælir
   b) tafla
   c) sýklalyf
   d) áburður

3) pharmacist
   a) læknir
   b) vítamín
   c) munnskol
   d) kortisón

4) injection
   a) insulin
   b) munnskol
   c) tafla
   d) innspýting

5) medicine
   a) innspýting
   b) apótek
   c) lyf
   d) tafla

6) dental floss
   a) tafla
   b) munnskol
   c) plástur
   d) áburður

7) cortisone
   a) kortisón
   b) innspýting
   c) pensilín
   d) lyf

8) bandage
   a) plástur
   b) læknir
   c) sýklalyf
   d) tafla

9) pill
   a) lyf
   b) apótek
   c) tafla
   d) plástur

10) laxative
   a) hægðalyf
   b) sýklalyf
   c) kortisón
   d) plástur

Word Quiz #94 - Pharmacy

Choose the best Icelandic word to match the English word.

1) dental floss
  a) lyf
  b) munnskol
  c) áburður
  d) apótek

2) injection
  a) apótek
  b) aspirin
  c) lyf
  d) innspýting

3) vitamin
  a) innspýting
  b) joð
  c) apótek
  d) vítamín

4) ointment
  a) læknir
  b) innspýting
  c) áburður
  d) tafla

5) prescription
  a) plástur
  b) sýklalyf
  c) lyfseðill
  d) munnskol

6) penicillin
  a) læknir
  b) sýklalyf
  c) hægðalyf
  d) pensilín

7) insulin
  a) pensilín
  b) tafla
  c) insulin
  d) lyfseðill

8) syrup
  a) munnskol
  b) innspýting
  c) insulin
  d) sýróp

9) medicine
  a) pensilín
  b) lyf
  c) plástur
  d) læknir

10) aspirin
  a) áburður
  b) munnskol
  c) aspirin
  d) plástur

Word Quiz #95 - Pharmacy

Choose the best Icelandic word to match the English word.

1) antibiotic
- a) lyf
- b) sýklalyf
- c) tafla
- d) áburður

2) laxative
- a) hitamælir
- b) hægðalyf
- c) insulin
- d) joð

3) thermometer
- a) hitamælir
- b) læknir
- c) aspirin
- d) kortisón

4) penicillin
- a) hitamælir
- b) aspirin
- c) pensilín
- d) apótek

5) tablet
- a) kortisón
- b) tafla
- c) hitamælir
- d) vítamín

6) dental floss
- a) tafla
- b) munnskol
- c) pensilín
- d) læknir

7) pharmacy
- a) pensilín
- b) kortisón
- c) apótek
- d) hitamælir

8) injection
- a) innspýting
- b) pensilín
- c) sýklalyf
- d) aspirin

9) cortisone
- a) læknir
- b) pensilín
- c) áburður
- d) kortisón

10) insulin
- a) læknir
- b) tafla
- c) sýklalyf
- d) insulin

Word Quiz #96 - Pharmacy

Choose the best Icelandic word to match the English word.

1) tablet
 a) lyf
 b) lyfseðill
 c) tafla
 d) sýklalyf

2) vitamin
 a) pensilín
 b) áburður
 c) vítamín
 d) plástur

3) ointment
 a) áburður
 b) tafla
 c) lyfseðill
 d) hægðalyf

4) cortisone
 a) sýróp
 b) kortisón
 c) plástur
 d) pensilín

5) bandage
 a) sýklalyf
 b) plástur
 c) hitamælir
 d) hægðalyf

6) insulin
 a) tafla
 b) insulin
 c) hitamælir
 d) læknir

7) laxative
 a) innspýting
 b) munnskol
 c) apótek
 d) hægðalyf

8) thermometer
 a) sýklalyf
 b) hitamælir
 c) apótek
 d) læknir

9) aspirin
 a) plástur
 b) læknir
 c) aspirin
 d) innspýting

10) medicine
 a) lyf
 b) innspýting
 c) plástur
 d) pensilín

Word Quiz #97 - Pharmacy

Choose the best Icelandic word to match the English word.

1) insulin
 a) joð
 b) insulin
 c) lyf
 d) pensilín

2) syrup
 a) munnskol
 b) sýróp
 c) vítamín
 d) áburður

3) cortisone
 a) lyf
 b) kortisón
 c) aspirin
 d) hitamælir

4) aspirin
 a) aspirin
 b) joð
 c) hægðalyf
 d) kortisón

5) dental floss
 a) pensilín
 b) læknir
 c) munnskol
 d) sýklalyf

6) pharmacist
 a) hitamælir
 b) munnskol
 c) læknir
 d) hægðalyf

7) iodine
 a) joð
 b) hitamælir
 c) áburður
 d) pensilín

8) bandage
 a) plástur
 b) lyfseðill
 c) joð
 d) tafla

9) prescription
 a) læknir
 b) lyfseðill
 c) plástur
 d) apótek

10) pill
 a) tafla
 b) sýróp
 c) apótek
 d) pensilín

Word Quiz #98 - Pharmacy

Choose the best Icelandic word to match the English word.

1) vitamin
 a) tafla
 b) vítamín
 c) munnskol
 d) pensilín

2) iodine
 a) kortisón
 b) aspirin
 c) joð
 d) plástur

3) prescription
 a) lyfseðill
 b) insulin
 c) áburður
 d) lyf

4) aspirin
 a) aspirin
 b) vítamín
 c) joð
 d) sýklalyf

5) pharmacist
 a) læknir
 b) aspirin
 c) tafla
 d) kortisón

6) dental floss
 a) munnskol
 b) lyf
 c) pensilín
 d) plástur

7) bandage
 a) plástur
 b) hitamælir
 c) joð
 d) sýróp

8) tablet
 a) læknir
 b) apótek
 c) tafla
 d) innspýting

9) syrup
 a) lyfseðill
 b) tafla
 c) pensilín
 d) sýróp

10) pharmacy
 a) apótek
 b) lyf
 c) pensilín
 d) lyfseðill

Word Quiz #99 - Pharmacy

Choose the best Icelandic word to match the English word.

1) tablet
a) munnskol
b) kortisón
c) tafla
d) lyfseðill

2) thermometer
a) hitamælir
b) læknir
c) hægðalyf
d) tafla

3) laxative
a) hægðalyf
b) insulin
c) áburður
d) lyfseðill

4) penicillin
a) tafla
b) pensilín
c) sýklalyf
d) insulin

5) pill
a) sýklalyf
b) kortisón
c) tafla
d) vítamín

6) cortisone
a) kortisón
b) pensilín
c) tafla
d) munnskol

7) dental floss
a) læknir
b) munnskol
c) pensilín
d) tafla

8) pharmacy
a) hitamælir
b) hægðalyf
c) sýklalyf
d) apótek

9) syrup
a) læknir
b) hægðalyf
c) sýróp
d) vítamín

10) iodine
a) tafla
b) joð
c) læknir
d) insulin

Word Quiz #100 - Pharmacy

Choose the best Icelandic word to match the English word.

1) bandage
 a) áburður
 b) joð
 c) innspýting
 d) plástur

2) insulin
 a) hitamælir
 b) munnskol
 c) sýróp
 d) insulin

3) prescription
 a) sýróp
 b) tafla
 c) lyfseðill
 d) aspirin

4) antibiotic
 a) sýklalyf
 b) innspýting
 c) plástur
 d) joð

5) ointment
 a) apótek
 b) tafla
 c) áburður
 d) sýróp

6) medicine
 a) hægðalyf
 b) sýróp
 c) tafla
 d) lyf

7) vitamin
 a) vítamín
 b) insulin
 c) apótek
 d) lyf

8) pharmacist
 a) munnskol
 b) tafla
 c) insulin
 d) læknir

9) penicillin
 a) innspýting
 b) joð
 c) apótek
 d) pensilín

10) aspirin
 a) aspirin
 b) sýklalyf
 c) lyfseðill
 d) munnskol

Word Quiz #101 - Places

Choose the best English word to match the Icelandic word.

1) Rússland
a) Portugal
b) Russia
c) Turkey
d) Denmark

2) Ísrael
a) United States
b) China
c) South America
d) Israel

3) Júgóslavía
a) Russia
b) Ireland
c) Yugoslavia
d) Finland

4) Morokkó
a) Switzerland
b) Algeria
c) Luxembourg
d) Morocco

5) Ítalía
a) Italy
b) Europe
c) Yugoslavia
d) Algeria

6) Svíþjóð
a) Finland
b) Sweden
c) Denmark
d) Austria

7) Holland
a) Netherlands
b) Morocco
c) Belgium
d) Europe

8) Sviss
a) Switzerland
b) Africa
c) South America
d) Finland

9) Kína
a) Finland
b) South Africa
c) China
d) England

10) Finnland
a) Russia
b) Algeria
c) Finland
d) Scotland

Word Quiz #102 - Places

Choose the best English word to match the Icelandic word.

1) Írland
  a) Ireland
  b) South Africa
  c) Greece
  d) Norway

2) Ísrael
  a) Europe
  b) England
  c) Israel
  d) Morocco

3) Kína
  a) Belgium
  b) China
  c) Italy
  d) Finland

4) Asía
  a) Asia
  b) Yugoslavia
  c) South America
  d) Finland

5) Kanada
  a) Africa
  b) Spain
  c) Canada
  d) Europe

6) Lúxemborg
  a) Israel
  b) Luxembourg
  c) Japan
  d) China

7) Grikkland
  a) Denmark
  b) China
  c) Greece
  d) Sweden

8) Frakkland
  a) Yugoslavia
  b) France
  c) Spain
  d) Norway

9) Suður Afríka
  a) South Africa
  b) Greece
  c) New Zealand
  d) Africa

10) Nýja Sjáland
  a) South America
  b) New Zealand
  c) Italy
  d) Sweden

Word Quiz #103 - Places

Choose the best English word to match the Icelandic word.

1) Ísrael
a) Portugal
b) Japan
c) Russia
d) Israel

2) Írland
a) France
b) North America
c) Great Britain
d) Ireland

3) Asía
a) Australia
b) Asia
c) Russia
d) Switzerland

4) Afríka
a) Australia
b) England
c) Yugoslavia
d) Africa

5) Suður Afríka
a) Israel
b) Germany
c) Algeria
d) South Africa

6) Norður Ameríka
a) Portugal
b) Germany
c) New Zealand
d) North America

7) Nýja Sjáland
a) Scotland
b) New Zealand
c) Greece
d) England

8) Evrópa
a) Europe
b) Asia
c) Tunisia
d) Japan

9) Tyrkland
a) Turkey
b) France
c) United States
d) Switzerland

10) Svíþjóð
a) Turkey
b) Sweden
c) South Africa
d) Switzerland

Word Quiz #104 - Places

Choose the best English word to match the Icelandic word.

1) Asía
 a) Sweden
 b) India
 c) Africa
 d) Asia

2) Tyrkland
 a) France
 b) Netherlands
 c) Algeria
 d) Turkey

3) Holland
 a) Africa
 b) Greece
 c) Netherlands
 d) Ireland

4) Suður Afríka
 a) India
 b) South Africa
 c) Sweden
 d) Morocco

5) Rússland
 a) Russia
 b) South Africa
 c) Norway
 d) Canada

6) Afríka
 a) Africa
 b) Slovenia
 c) Finland
 d) Italy

7) Kanada
 a) Canada
 b) South Africa
 c) Great Britain
 d) Morocco

8) Algería
 a) Morocco
 b) Italy
 c) France
 d) Algeria

9) Suður Ameríka
 a) Germany
 b) Europe
 c) South America
 d) Switzerland

10) Ísrael
 a) Great Britain
 b) Italy
 c) Israel
 d) Spain

Word Quiz #105 - Places

Choose the best English word to match the Icelandic word.

1) Júgóslavía
a) Yugoslavia
b) South Africa
c) Great Britain
d) Morocco

2) England
a) Ireland
b) South America
c) India
d) England

3) Austurríki
a) Austria
b) Netherlands
c) Ireland
d) North America

4) Kína
a) North America
b) Wales
c) China
d) Europe

5) Slóvenía
a) Slovenia
b) India
c) Portugal
d) Sweden

6) Suður Ameríka
a) Sweden
b) Netherlands
c) South America
d) Norway

7) Portúgal
a) Canada
b) Russia
c) Germany
d) Portugal

8) Bandaríkin
a) Belgium
b) Asia
c) Switzerland
d) United States

9) Spánn
a) Europe
b) Australia
c) Spain
d) Luxembourg

10) Danmörk
a) North America
b) Denmark
c) Belgium
d) Netherlands

Word Quiz #106 - Places

Choose the best English word to match the Icelandic word.

1) Spánn
a) Spain
b) Morocco
c) Africa
d) United States

2) Noregur
a) Greece
b) Norway
c) Israel
d) North America

3) Slóvenía
a) Slovenia
b) India
c) Luxembourg
d) Norway

4) Ástralía
a) Sweden
b) Scotland
c) Morocco
d) Australia

5) Ísrael
a) South Africa
b) Yugoslavia
c) Israel
d) Europe

6) Danmörk
a) Norway
b) South America
c) Denmark
d) China

7) Írland
a) Russia
b) Ireland
c) Israel
d) Germany

8) Evrópa
a) Morocco
b) Austria
c) Great Britain
d) Europe

9) England
a) England
b) Yugoslavia
c) Canada
d) Japan

10) Holland
a) Netherlands
b) Great Britain
c) New Zealand
d) Greece

Word Quiz #107 - Places

Choose the best English word to match the Icelandic word.

1) Skotland
 a) Scotland
 b) Finland
 c) Italy
 d) Europe

2) Wales
 a) Wales
 b) Denmark
 c) Norway
 d) Turkey

3) Ísrael
 a) Morocco
 b) Scotland
 c) Israel
 d) Turkey

4) Holland
 a) Netherlands
 b) China
 c) Australia
 d) Algeria

5) Júgóslavía
 a) Finland
 b) Yugoslavia
 c) Europe
 d) Asia

6) Írland
 a) Africa
 b) Great Britain
 c) Ireland
 d) Canada

7) Kína
 a) Greece
 b) Germany
 c) China
 d) Netherlands

8) Tyrkland
 a) Turkey
 b) Greece
 c) North America
 d) Germany

9) Portúgal
 a) Australia
 b) Portugal
 c) China
 d) Tunisia

10) Afríka
 a) Africa
 b) Russia
 c) South Africa
 d) Belgium

Word Quiz #108 - Places

Choose the best English word to match the Icelandic word.

1) Suður Afríka
  a) South Africa
  b) Japan
  c) Greece
  d) Finland

2) Suður Ameríka
  a) Algeria
  b) Turkey
  c) South America
  d) Tunisia

3) Austurríki
  a) Wales
  b) India
  c) Austria
  d) Finland

4) Kanada
  a) Sweden
  b) Greece
  c) Canada
  d) North America

5) England
  a) Slovenia
  b) England
  c) Africa
  d) United States

6) Ástralía
  a) Portugal
  b) Algeria
  c) Australia
  d) Africa

7) Ítalía
  a) Tunisia
  b) Italy
  c) Norway
  d) Asia

8) Frakkland
  a) Yugoslavia
  b) France
  c) Russia
  d) Slovenia

9) Þýskaland
  a) United States
  b) Finland
  c) Spain
  d) Germany

10) Sviss
  a) Japan
  b) Luxembourg
  c) Algeria
  d) Switzerland

Word Quiz #109 - Places

Choose the best English word to match the Icelandic word.

1) Ísrael
   a) India
   b) Greece
   c) Great Britain
   d) Israel

2) Tyrkland
   a) North America
   b) Germany
   c) Turkey
   d) South Africa

3) Portúgal
   a) Portugal
   b) United States
   c) Europe
   d) Japan

4) Holland
   a) Netherlands
   b) Yugoslavia
   c) Great Britain
   d) Algeria

5) Írland
   a) Ireland
   b) England
   c) Italy
   d) Algeria

6) Noregur
   a) India
   b) Norway
   c) South America
   d) Great Britain

7) Bretland
   a) Israel
   b) Africa
   c) Switzerland
   d) Great Britain

8) Rússland
   a) Sweden
   b) Canada
   c) Japan
   d) Russia

9) Skotland
   a) Africa
   b) Russia
   c) New Zealand
   d) Scotland

10) England
   a) Italy
   b) Greece
   c) England
   d) Africa

Word Quiz #110 - Places

Choose the best English word to match the Icelandic word.

1) Afríka
 a) Africa
 b) Israel
 c) Belgium
 d) Yugoslavia

2) Evrópa
 a) United States
 b) Europe
 c) England
 d) Russia

3) England
 a) England
 b) Wales
 c) South Africa
 d) Great Britain

4) Suður Afríka
 a) Canada
 b) South Africa
 c) Asia
 d) Switzerland

5) Bandaríkin
 a) United States
 b) Japan
 c) Denmark
 d) Russia

6) Ísrael
 a) South America
 b) Japan
 c) Slovenia
 d) Israel

7) Bretland
 a) India
 b) Spain
 c) Yugoslavia
 d) Great Britain

8) Svíþjóð
 a) South America
 b) South Africa
 c) Sweden
 d) Turkey

9) Frakkland
 a) France
 b) England
 c) Austria
 d) Great Britain

10) Austurríki
 a) Denmark
 b) Austria
 c) Asia
 d) Greece

Word Quiz #111 - Places

Choose the best English word to match the Icelandic word.

1) Ísrael
  a) Australia
  b) Israel
  c) Wales
  d) Tunisia

2) Finnland
  a) Ireland
  b) Finland
  c) India
  d) Luxembourg

3) Túnis
  a) Luxembourg
  b) Tunisia
  c) India
  d) Spain

4) Rússland
  a) Spain
  b) Europe
  c) Russia
  d) Tunisia

5) Portúgal
  a) Israel
  b) Italy
  c) Portugal
  d) Turkey

6) Svíþjóð
  a) Slovenia
  b) Sweden
  c) Denmark
  d) Africa

7) Algería
  a) Algeria
  b) Sweden
  c) South America
  d) Russia

8) Júgóslavía
  a) Netherlands
  b) New Zealand
  c) Germany
  d) Yugoslavia

9) Suður Ameríka
  a) Asia
  b) China
  c) Germany
  d) South America

10) Frakkland
  a) Morocco
  b) England
  c) France
  d) Denmark

Word Quiz #112 - Places

Choose the best English word to match the Icelandic word.

1) Kína
a) Great Britain
b) South America
c) China
d) Yugoslavia

2) Indland
a) India
b) Luxembourg
c) Slovenia
d) Sweden

3) Asía
a) North America
b) Netherlands
c) Luxembourg
d) Asia

4) Þýskaland
a) Spain
b) Germany
c) Tunisia
d) Austria

5) Algería
a) Sweden
b) Austria
c) Algeria
d) New Zealand

6) England
a) England
b) Greece
c) Spain
d) Japan

7) Noregur
a) Wales
b) Portugal
c) Norway
d) Canada

8) Bretland
a) Great Britain
b) Europe
c) Yugoslavia
d) Austria

9) Finnland
a) Finland
b) Scotland
c) Luxembourg
d) Italy

10) Írland
a) Ireland
b) Norway
c) Sweden
d) North America

Word Quiz #113 - Places

Choose the best English word to match the Icelandic word.

1) Suður Ameríka
   a) Asia
   b) South America
   c) Austria
   d) Morocco

2) England
   a) England
   b) Turkey
   c) United States
   d) Norway

3) Svíþjóð
   a) Tunisia
   b) China
   c) Wales
   d) Sweden

4) Wales
   a) Wales
   b) Slovenia
   c) Belgium
   d) Austria

5) Sviss
   a) Japan
   b) Switzerland
   c) Europe
   d) South Africa

6) Rússland
   a) Denmark
   b) Norway
   c) Russia
   d) Slovenia

7) Júgóslavía
   a) Wales
   b) Austria
   c) Norway
   d) Yugoslavia

8) Bandaríkin
   a) Asia
   b) Luxembourg
   c) United States
   d) Israel

9) Þýskaland
   a) Sweden
   b) Germany
   c) India
   d) Ireland

10) Portúgal
   a) Portugal
   b) Greece
   c) England
   d) Algeria

Word Quiz #114 - Places

Choose the best Icelandic word to match the English word.

1) Yugoslavia
- a) England
- b) Asía
- c) Júgóslavía
- d) Suður Ameríka

2) Greece
- a) Rússland
- b) Afríka
- c) Grikkland
- d) Spánn

3) New Zealand
- a) Nýja Sjáland
- b) Spánn
- c) Frakkland
- d) Algería

4) Africa
- a) Afríka
- b) Kína
- c) Asía
- d) Holland

5) China
- a) Kína
- b) England
- c) Ástralía
- d) Lúxemborg

6) Spain
- a) Norður Ameríka
- b) Evrópa
- c) Túnis
- d) Spánn

7) India
- a) Indland
- b) Danmörk
- c) Portúgal
- d) Kína

8) Austria
- a) Bretland
- b) Júgóslavía
- c) Austurríki
- d) England

9) Canada
- a) Belgía
- b) Ísrael
- c) Slóvenía
- d) Kanada

10) Norway
- a) Þýskaland
- b) Suður Afríka
- c) Svíþjóð
- d) Noregur

Word Quiz #115 - Places

Choose the best Icelandic word to match the English word.

1) Austria
 a) Túnis
 b) Írland
 c) Austurríki
 d) Þýskaland

2) Russia
 a) Kanada
 b) Noregur
 c) Spánn
 d) Rússland

3) Portugal
 a) Bretland
 b) Sviss
 c) Portúgal
 d) Evrópa

4) New Zealand
 a) Finnland
 b) Nýja Sjáland
 c) Kína
 d) Slóvenía

5) India
 a) Asía
 b) Belgía
 c) Indland
 d) Finnland

6) Australia
 a) Ástralía
 b) Grikkland
 c) Noregur
 d) Bretland

7) Algeria
 a) Portúgal
 b) Algería
 c) Rússland
 d) Grikkland

8) China
 a) Kína
 b) Suður Afríka
 c) Austurríki
 d) Bretland

9) South America
 a) Tyrkland
 b) Danmörk
 c) Noregur
 d) Suður Ameríka

10) Ireland
 a) Portúgal
 b) Austurríki
 c) Holland
 d) Írland

Word Quiz #116 - Places

Choose the best Icelandic word to match the English word.

1) Wales
 a) Wales
 b) Túnis
 c) Noregur
 d) Suður Afríka

2) Russia
 a) Rússland
 b) Bandaríkin
 c) Algería
 d) Írland

3) China
 a) Algería
 b) Slóvenía
 c) Nýja Sjáland
 d) Kína

4) Italy
 a) Suður Ameríka
 b) Frakkland
 c) Algería
 d) Ítalía

5) North America
 a) Kanada
 b) Algería
 c) Asía
 d) Norður Ameríka

6) New Zealand
 a) Tyrkland
 b) Bretland
 c) Morokkó
 d) Nýja Sjáland

7) Austria
 a) Nýja Sjáland
 b) Asía
 c) Austurríki
 d) Ítalía

8) Switzerland
 a) Þýskaland
 b) Austurríki
 c) Danmörk
 d) Sviss

9) Sweden
 a) Svíþjóð
 b) Ítalía
 c) Tyrkland
 d) England

10) Africa
 a) Finnland
 b) Afríka
 c) England
 d) Norður Ameríka

Word Quiz #117 - Places

Choose the best Icelandic word to match the English word.

1) South America
- a) Belgía
- b) Skotland
- c) Suður Ameríka
- d) England

2) New Zealand
- a) Morokkó
- b) Spánn
- c) Ítalía
- d) Nýja Sjáland

3) Ireland
- a) Írland
- b) England
- c) Austurríki
- d) Wales

4) Switzerland
- a) Slóvenía
- b) Sviss
- c) Þýskaland
- d) Holland

5) Belgium
- a) Bandaríkin
- b) Ástralía
- c) Belgía
- d) Holland

6) South Africa
- a) Túnis
- b) Svíþjóð
- c) Finnland
- d) Suður Afríka

7) Morocco
- a) Grikkland
- b) England
- c) Slóvenía
- d) Morokkó

8) Tunisia
- a) Tyrkland
- b) Morokkó
- c) Svíþjóð
- d) Túnis

9) Germany
- a) Þýskaland
- b) Svíþjóð
- c) Írland
- d) Suður Ameríka

10) Africa
- a) Skotland
- b) Austurríki
- c) Afríka
- d) Ástralía

Word Quiz #118 - Places

Choose the best Icelandic word to match the English word.

1) Italy
  a) Portúgal
  b) Tyrkland
  c) Ítalía
  d) Suður Afríka

2) Yugoslavia
  a) Nýja Sjáland
  b) Þýskaland
  c) Júgóslavía
  d) England

3) Scotland
  a) Bandaríkin
  b) Frakkland
  c) Skotland
  d) Morokkó

4) Great Britain
  a) Spánn
  b) Wales
  c) Noregur
  d) Bretland

5) Morocco
  a) Holland
  b) Morokkó
  c) Túnis
  d) Wales

6) Germany
  a) Slóvenía
  b) Kanada
  c) Þýskaland
  d) Afríka

7) Finland
  a) Portúgal
  b) Finnland
  c) Suður Afríka
  d) Svíþjóð

8) Turkey
  a) Tyrkland
  b) Þýskaland
  c) Júgóslavía
  d) Túnis

9) Luxembourg
  a) Spánn
  b) Asía
  c) Skotland
  d) Lúxemborg

10) Portugal
  a) Belgía
  b) Portúgal
  c) Tyrkland
  d) Afríka

Word Quiz #119 - Places

Choose the best Icelandic word to match the English word.

1) Sweden
a) Írland
b) Svíþjóð
c) Morokkó
d) Holland

2) South America
a) Wales
b) Nýja Sjáland
c) Suður Ameríka
d) Japan

3) Italy
a) Bandaríkin
b) Grikkland
c) Ítalía
d) Morokkó

4) Algeria
a) Suður Afríka
b) Kína
c) Algería
d) Portúgal

5) India
a) Noregur
b) Írland
c) Indland
d) Sviss

6) Portugal
a) Danmörk
b) Lúxemborg
c) Júgóslavía
d) Portúgal

7) Great Britain
a) Austurríki
b) Slóvenía
c) Bretland
d) Suður Afríka

8) Wales
a) Lúxemborg
b) Wales
c) Afríka
d) England

9) Canada
a) Ástralía
b) Júgóslavía
c) Kanada
d) Skotland

10) North America
a) Norður Ameríka
b) Noregur
c) Portúgal
d) Lúxemborg

Word Quiz #120 - Places

Choose the best Icelandic word to match the English word.

1) Norway
  a) Wales
  b) Kína
  c) Slóvenía
  d) Noregur

2) Algeria
  a) Algería
  b) Finnland
  c) Tyrkland
  d) Holland

3) Wales
  a) Írland
  b) Norður Ameríka
  c) Þýskaland
  d) Wales

4) Italy
  a) England
  b) Finnland
  c) Ítalía
  d) Wales

5) Luxembourg
  a) Túnis
  b) Portúgal
  c) Afríka
  d) Lúxemborg

6) Canada
  a) Kanada
  b) Danmörk
  c) Nýja Sjáland
  d) Japan

7) Switzerland
  a) Skotland
  b) Portúgal
  c) Sviss
  d) Tyrkland

8) Australia
  a) Ástralía
  b) Lúxemborg
  c) Ísrael
  d) Frakkland

9) Germany
  a) Þýskaland
  b) Júgóslavía
  c) Ísrael
  d) Morokkó

10) Africa
  a) Morokkó
  b) Asía
  c) Rússland
  d) Afríka

Word Quiz #121 - Places

Choose the best Icelandic word to match the English word.

1) North America
a) Portúgal
b) Evrópa
c) Indland
d) Norður Ameríka

2) Russia
a) Rússland
b) Kína
c) Þýskaland
d) Portúgal

3) China
a) Noregur
b) Nýja Sjáland
c) Kína
d) Wales

4) Algeria
a) Bretland
b) Frakkland
c) Algería
d) Sviss

5) Turkey
a) Sviss
b) Indland
c) Morokkó
d) Tyrkland

6) Tunisia
a) Túnis
b) Rússland
c) Frakkland
d) Skotland

7) Ireland
a) Írland
b) Ítalía
c) Bandaríkin
d) Norður Ameríka

8) Yugoslavia
a) Austurríki
b) Írland
c) Júgóslavía
d) Ítalía

9) Finland
a) Finnland
b) Lúxemborg
c) Slóvenía
d) Wales

10) Wales
a) Rússland
b) Bandaríkin
c) Nýja Sjáland
d) Wales

Word Quiz #122 - Places

Choose the best Icelandic word to match the English word.

1) North America
a) Ísrael
b) Suður Ameríka
c) Spánn
d) Norður Ameríka

2) Sweden
a) Portúgal
b) Ísrael
c) Noregur
d) Svíþjóð

3) Europe
a) Kanada
b) Belgía
c) Svíþjóð
d) Evrópa

4) Belgium
a) Algería
b) Ítalía
c) Indland
d) Belgía

5) Tunisia
a) Suður Ameríka
b) Túnis
c) Holland
d) Asía

6) Luxembourg
a) Lúxemborg
b) Túnis
c) England
d) Japan

7) Germany
a) Ástralía
b) Skotland
c) Tyrkland
d) Þýskaland

8) Switzerland
a) England
b) Írland
c) Wales
d) Sviss

9) South America
a) Indland
b) Suður Ameríka
c) Frakkland
d) Danmörk

10) Turkey
a) Morokkó
b) Austurríki
c) Tyrkland
d) Írland

Word Quiz #123 - Places

Choose the best Icelandic word to match the English word.

1) South Africa
- a) Wales
- b) Indland
- c) Grikkland
- d) Suður Afríka

2) Belgium
- a) Rússland
- b) Japan
- c) Grikkland
- d) Belgía

3) England
- a) England
- b) Írland
- c) Túnis
- d) Afríka

4) Scotland
- a) Ítalía
- b) Kanada
- c) Ísrael
- d) Skotland

5) Netherlands
- a) Holland
- b) Bandaríkin
- c) Indland
- d) Wales

6) Africa
- a) England
- b) Afríka
- c) Slóvenía
- d) Suður Afríka

7) Yugoslavia
- a) Austurríki
- b) Evrópa
- c) Kanada
- d) Júgóslavía

8) Tunisia
- a) Tyrkland
- b) Túnis
- c) Suður Ameríka
- d) Írland

9) Asia
- a) Túnis
- b) Evrópa
- c) Skotland
- d) Asía

10) North America
- a) Þýskaland
- b) Skotland
- c) Norður Ameríka
- d) Wales

Word Quiz #124 - Places

Choose the best Icelandic word to match the English word.

1) South America
a) Slóvenía
b) Suður Ameríka
c) Kína
d) Danmörk

2) Turkey
a) Noregur
b) Kanada
c) Slóvenía
d) Tyrkland

3) India
a) Indland
b) England
c) Noregur
d) Belgía

4) France
a) Frakkland
b) Evrópa
c) Túnis
d) Indland

5) United States
a) Ísrael
b) Spánn
c) Þýskaland
d) Bandaríkin

6) Denmark
a) Danmörk
b) Írland
c) Portúgal
d) Indland

7) Asia
a) Afríka
b) Nýja Sjáland
c) Asía
d) Ísrael

8) Africa
a) Belgía
b) Spánn
c) Bretland
d) Afríka

9) Scotland
a) Skotland
b) Danmörk
c) Indland
d) Ástralía

10) Russia
a) Wales
b) Rússland
c) Suður Ameríka
d) Grikkland

Word Quiz #125 - Places

Choose the best Icelandic word to match the English word.

1) Europe
   a) Ítalía
   b) Evrópa
   c) Svíþjóð
   d) Rússland

2) Slovenia
   a) Grikkland
   b) Belgía
   c) Portúgal
   d) Slóvenía

3) Netherlands
   a) Holland
   b) Portúgal
   c) Lúxemborg
   d) Evrópa

4) Asia
   a) Holland
   b) Asía
   c) Wales
   d) Tyrkland

5) Greece
   a) Bretland
   b) Grikkland
   c) Norður Ameríka
   d) Algería

6) Germany
   a) Holland
   b) Svíþjóð
   c) Bandaríkin
   d) Þýskaland

7) Japan
   a) Júgóslavía
   b) Japan
   c) Ítalía
   d) Þýskaland

8) South Africa
   a) Suður Afríka
   b) Indland
   c) Þýskaland
   d) Grikkland

9) Finland
   a) Bretland
   b) Morokkó
   c) Finnland
   d) Kína

10) Great Britain
   a) Spánn
   b) Danmörk
   c) Bretland
   d) Suður Ameríka

Word Quiz #126 - Postal

Choose the best English word to match the Icelandic word.

1) bréf
a) letter
b) to send
c) post office
d) import

2) umslag
a) postman
b) courier
c) export
d) envelope

3) að skrifa
a) to write
b) import
c) to send
d) money order

4) póstur
a) money order
b) post
c) note
d) package

5) peningasending
a) postage stamp
b) airmail
c) to write
d) money order

6) boðberi
a) envelope
b) registered letter
c) post
d) courier

7) afgreiðslumaður
a) reply
b) clerk
c) postage stamp
d) address

8) að bíða
a) clerk
b) to wait
c) reply
d) postman

9) sendandi
a) sender
b) money order
c) letter
d) export

10) að senda
a) reply
b) to send
c) export
d) letter

Word Quiz #127 - Postal

Choose the best English word to match the Icelandic word.

1) skráð bréf
   a) to wait
   b) airmail
   c) sender
   d) registered letter

2) afgreiðslumaður
   a) printed item
   b) clerk
   c) letter
   d) envelope

3) bréf
   a) sender
   b) courier
   c) to write
   d) letter

4) að deila
   a) postage stamp
   b) sender
   c) to send
   d) to post

5) pakki
   a) export
   b) note
   c) package
   d) sender

6) innflutningur
   a) money order
   b) clerk
   c) letter
   d) import

7) boðberi
   a) post office
   b) postman
   c) courier
   d) envelope

8) sendandi
   a) letterbox
   b) sender
   c) postage stamp
   d) registered letter

9) bréfberi
   a) note
   b) to write
   c) postman
   d) to send

10) flugpóstur
   a) post office
   b) courier
   c) money order
   d) airmail

Word Quiz #128 - Postal

Choose the best English word to match the Icelandic word.

1) heimilisfang
   a) letterbox
   b) to send
   c) envelope
   d) address

2) póstur
   a) airmail
   b) package
   c) post
   d) postman

3) peningasending
   a) money order
   b) sender
   c) reply
   d) postage stamp

4) að senda
   a) clerk
   b) to write
   c) sender
   d) to send

5) svar
   a) reply
   b) courier
   c) import
   d) postman

6) að bíða
   a) to wait
   b) post office
   c) import
   d) to send

7) innflutningur
   a) import
   b) money order
   c) courier
   d) postman

8) póstbox
   a) letterbox
   b) post office
   c) letter
   d) note

9) flugpóstur
   a) letterbox
   b) to wait
   c) airmail
   d) package

10) afgreiðslumaður
   a) post
   b) to send
   c) post office
   d) clerk

Word Quiz #129 - Postal

Choose the best English word to match the Icelandic word.

1) afgreiðslumaður
  a) to wait
  b) clerk
  c) letterbox
  d) post

2) skráð bréf
  a) registered letter
  b) letter
  c) postman
  d) money order

3) boðberi
  a) export
  b) to post
  c) registered letter
  d) courier

4) peningasending
  a) export
  b) money order
  c) letter
  d) address

5) innflutningur
  a) envelope
  b) note
  c) import
  d) package

6) að senda
  a) money order
  b) to send
  c) postage stamp
  d) package

7) póstur
  a) envelope
  b) note
  c) post
  d) to send

8) að deila
  a) export
  b) note
  c) to post
  d) registered letter

9) að skrifa
  a) to write
  b) post
  c) envelope
  d) airmail

10) prentað bréf
  a) postman
  b) courier
  c) printed item
  d) envelope

Word Quiz #130 - Postal

Choose the best English word to match the Icelandic word.

1) heimilisfang
   a) address
   b) to write
   c) envelope
   d) courier

2) innflutningur
   a) note
   b) package
   c) import
   d) clerk

3) pósthús
   a) postage stamp
   b) reply
   c) address
   d) post office

4) sendandi
   a) postage stamp
   b) courier
   c) export
   d) sender

5) að senda
   a) to post
   b) money order
   c) to send
   d) export

6) prentað bréf
   a) reply
   b) money order
   c) printed item
   d) letter

7) afgreiðslumaður
   a) clerk
   b) to post
   c) money order
   d) to write

8) að skrifa
   a) to post
   b) note
   c) to write
   d) money order

9) flugpóstur
   a) airmail
   b) to write
   c) package
   d) clerk

10) bréf
   a) airmail
   b) printed item
   c) note
   d) clerk

Word Quiz #131 - Postal

Choose the best English word to match the Icelandic word.

1) afgreiðslumaður
 a) clerk
 b) courier
 c) letter
 d) postage stamp

2) bréf
 a) note
 b) letter
 c) reply
 d) money order

3) pakki
 a) reply
 b) postman
 c) post
 d) package

4) bréf
 a) airmail
 b) money order
 c) note
 d) import

5) svar
 a) postman
 b) export
 c) letterbox
 d) reply

6) póstbox
 a) post office
 b) envelope
 c) letterbox
 d) post

7) peningasending
 a) printed item
 b) registered letter
 c) money order
 d) export

8) að deila
 a) reply
 b) import
 c) to post
 d) postage stamp

9) heimilisfang
 a) sender
 b) post
 c) address
 d) postman

10) skráð bréf
 a) sender
 b) package
 c) to write
 d) registered letter

Word Quiz #132 - Postal

Choose the best English word to match the Icelandic word.

1) umslag
   a) envelope
   b) address
   c) registered letter
   d) post office

2) sendandi
   a) airmail
   b) sender
   c) to write
   d) registered letter

3) pósthús
   a) printed item
   b) post office
   c) import
   d) post

4) að senda
   a) letter
   b) import
   c) to send
   d) to write

5) að skrifa
   a) to post
   b) to write
   c) postman
   d) envelope

6) póstbox
   a) sender
   b) letterbox
   c) to write
   d) package

7) svar
   a) export
   b) reply
   c) import
   d) sender

8) skráð bréf
   a) to write
   b) registered letter
   c) post
   d) package

9) flugpóstur
   a) airmail
   b) money order
   c) postman
   d) postage stamp

10) pakki
   a) post
   b) printed item
   c) package
   d) to post

Word Quiz #133 - Postal

Choose the best English word to match the Icelandic word.

1) pósthús
   a) reply
   b) post office
   c) package
   d) address

2) bréf
   a) airmail
   b) printed item
   c) to post
   d) note

3) póstur
   a) to wait
   b) to send
   c) post
   d) sender

4) frímerki
   a) import
   b) reply
   c) clerk
   d) postage stamp

5) póstbox
   a) printed item
   b) letterbox
   c) to send
   d) reply

6) að senda
   a) address
   b) to send
   c) post
   d) export

7) skráð bréf
   a) to wait
   b) registered letter
   c) courier
   d) postage stamp

8) peningasending
   a) import
   b) to post
   c) money order
   d) note

9) að deila
   a) sender
   b) post
   c) to post
   d) registered letter

10) bréfberi
   a) postman
   b) printed item
   c) postage stamp
   d) registered letter

Word Quiz #134 - Postal

Choose the best English word to match the Icelandic word.

1) bréf
  a) letter
  b) to send
  c) reply
  d) to write

2) pakki
  a) package
  b) money order
  c) export
  d) sender

3) að skrifa
  a) to write
  b) package
  c) registered letter
  d) to send

4) boðberi
  a) address
  b) courier
  c) airmail
  d) reply

5) innflutningur
  a) letter
  b) airmail
  c) post office
  d) import

6) að senda
  a) to send
  b) export
  c) to post
  d) money order

7) póstbox
  a) package
  b) letterbox
  c) clerk
  d) to post

8) skráð bréf
  a) letterbox
  b) registered letter
  c) letter
  d) sender

9) útfluttningur
  a) note
  b) export
  c) registered letter
  d) to write

10) póstur
  a) post
  b) to write
  c) to post
  d) money order

Word Quiz #135 - Postal

Choose the best English word to match the Icelandic word.

1) að deila
 a) courier
 b) to post
 c) sender
 d) printed item

2) skráð bréf
 a) to post
 b) clerk
 c) to wait
 d) registered letter

3) flugpóstur
 a) airmail
 b) post
 c) money order
 d) clerk

4) bréfberi
 a) courier
 b) to wait
 c) postman
 d) postage stamp

5) heimilisfang
 a) printed item
 b) to write
 c) address
 d) clerk

6) pakki
 a) printed item
 b) postage stamp
 c) registered letter
 d) package

7) svar
 a) reply
 b) registered letter
 c) postman
 d) airmail

8) pósthús
 a) post office
 b) post
 c) note
 d) to post

9) afgreiðslumaður
 a) clerk
 b) post office
 c) courier
 d) letter

10) að skrifa
 a) clerk
 b) to write
 c) address
 d) money order

Word Quiz #136 - Postal

Choose the best English word to match the Icelandic word.

1) innflutningur
a) reply
b) import
c) courier
d) sender

2) póstbox
a) letterbox
b) to send
c) courier
d) airmail

3) frímerki
a) to send
b) letter
c) postman
d) postage stamp

4) heimilisfang
a) to post
b) airmail
c) address
d) import

5) prentað bréf
a) printed item
b) to post
c) envelope
d) export

6) útfluttningur
a) to send
b) letter
c) sender
d) export

7) skráð bréf
a) clerk
b) note
c) registered letter
d) postage stamp

8) að deila
a) to send
b) address
c) printed item
d) to post

9) að bíða
a) envelope
b) letter
c) to wait
d) post

10) sendandi
a) post office
b) letterbox
c) sender
d) to wait

Word Quiz #137 - Postal

Choose the best English word to match the Icelandic word.

1) flugpóstur
- a) registered letter
- b) airmail
- c) export
- d) to post

2) bréfberi
- a) postage stamp
- b) postman
- c) money order
- d) to send

3) bréf
- a) note
- b) printed item
- c) letter
- d) import

4) boðberi
- a) letter
- b) package
- c) courier
- d) to wait

5) að senda
- a) airmail
- b) note
- c) import
- d) to send

6) peningasending
- a) courier
- b) envelope
- c) address
- d) money order

7) póstur
- a) postman
- b) clerk
- c) post
- d) envelope

8) pósthús
- a) import
- b) post office
- c) post
- d) sender

9) innflutningur
- a) envelope
- b) letter
- c) import
- d) printed item

10) pakki
- a) to write
- b) letterbox
- c) package
- d) post office

Word Quiz #138 - Postal

Choose the best English word to match the Icelandic word.

1) svar
  a) airmail
  b) to write
  c) letter
  d) reply

2) útfluttningur
  a) address
  b) export
  c) to send
  d) to post

3) bréfberi
  a) postman
  b) to write
  c) clerk
  d) letterbox

4) bréf
  a) letter
  b) reply
  c) to send
  d) to wait

5) sendandi
  a) postman
  b) package
  c) sender
  d) printed item

6) umslag
  a) envelope
  b) money order
  c) clerk
  d) postage stamp

7) að deila
  a) to post
  b) package
  c) to send
  d) letter

8) innflutningur
  a) import
  b) money order
  c) note
  d) to write

9) flugpóstur
  a) to post
  b) money order
  c) airmail
  d) package

10) skráð bréf
  a) envelope
  b) letter
  c) registered letter
  d) package

Word Quiz #139 - Postal

Choose the best Icelandic word to match the English word.

1) import
 a) umslag
 b) útfluttningur
 c) að senda
 d) innflutningur

2) letter
 a) pakki
 b) sendandi
 c) að bíða
 d) bréf

3) printed item
 a) pósthús
 b) boðberi
 c) prentað bréf
 d) að senda

4) to send
 a) bréfberi
 b) að skrifa
 c) að senda
 d) afgreiðslumaður

5) clerk
 a) póstur
 b) peningasending
 c) afgreiðslumaður
 d) póstbox

6) letterbox
 a) pósthús
 b) póstbox
 c) pakki
 d) innflutningur

7) export
 a) heimilisfang
 b) útfluttningur
 c) boðberi
 d) pakki

8) registered letter
 a) heimilisfang
 b) bréf
 c) skráð bréf
 d) peningasending

9) to wait
 a) að bíða
 b) bréf
 c) bréfberi
 d) póstbox

10) post office
 a) bréf
 b) bréfberi
 c) pósthús
 d) skráð bréf

Word Quiz #140 - Postal

Choose the best Icelandic word to match the English word.

1) to post
 a) bréfberi
 b) að deila
 c) boðberi
 d) afgreiðslumaður

2) postman
 a) innflutningur
 b) að deila
 c) peningasending
 d) bréfberi

3) postage stamp
 a) innflutningur
 b) frímerki
 c) prentað bréf
 d) að senda

4) sender
 a) að deila
 b) sendandi
 c) heimilisfang
 d) peningasending

5) address
 a) póstur
 b) heimilisfang
 c) að senda
 d) að deila

6) registered letter
 a) að deila
 b) skráð bréf
 c) póstbox
 d) prentað bréf

7) import
 a) útfluttningur
 b) skráð bréf
 c) innflutningur
 d) flugpóstur

8) letter
 a) sendandi
 b) bréf
 c) að senda
 d) boðberi

9) post office
 a) sendandi
 b) að skrifa
 c) skráð bréf
 d) pósthús

10) post
 a) pósthús
 b) póstur
 c) útfluttningur
 d) afgreiðslumaður

Word Quiz #141 - Postal

Choose the best Icelandic word to match the English word.

1) import
a) frímerki
b) svar
c) innflutningur
d) pakki

2) money order
a) peningasending
b) að deila
c) póstur
d) bréf

3) airmail
a) flugpóstur
b) póstur
c) bréf
d) boðberi

4) postage stamp
a) að bíða
b) póstbox
c) peningasending
d) frímerki

5) printed item
a) póstbox
b) útfluttningur
c) frímerki
d) prentað bréf

6) clerk
a) bréf
b) póstbox
c) pakki
d) afgreiðslumaður

7) address
a) heimilisfang
b) pakki
c) umslag
d) að bíða

8) package
a) bréf
b) pakki
c) bréfberi
d) póstur

9) letter
a) flugpóstur
b) pakki
c) bréf
d) að senda

10) to post
a) að deila
b) póstbox
c) að senda
d) flugpóstur

Word Quiz #142 - Postal

Choose the best Icelandic word to match the English word.

1) clerk
 a) sendandi
 b) að bíða
 c) flugpóstur
 d) afgreiðslumaður

2) money order
 a) bréfberi
 b) frímerki
 c) pósthús
 d) peningasending

3) to send
 a) póstur
 b) að senda
 c) bréfberi
 d) boðberi

4) reply
 a) flugpóstur
 b) bréf
 c) póstbox
 d) svar

5) to post
 a) umslag
 b) að deila
 c) bréfberi
 d) pósthús

6) letter
 a) innflutningur
 b) póstur
 c) bréf
 d) útfluttningur

7) courier
 a) sendandi
 b) bréfberi
 c) boðberi
 d) póstur

8) address
 a) að deila
 b) póstbox
 c) heimilisfang
 d) flugpóstur

9) envelope
 a) að deila
 b) umslag
 c) flugpóstur
 d) peningasending

10) sender
 a) bréfberi
 b) afgreiðslumaður
 c) sendandi
 d) að skrifa

Word Quiz #143 - Postal

Choose the best Icelandic word to match the English word.

1) sender
  a) að skrifa
  b) útfluttningur
  c) sendandi
  d) boðberi

2) letter
  a) skráð bréf
  b) flugpóstur
  c) bréf
  d) umslag

3) to wait
  a) prentað bréf
  b) að bíða
  c) svar
  d) bréf

4) package
  a) heimilisfang
  b) boðberi
  c) póstbox
  d) pakki

5) money order
  a) innflutningur
  b) peningasending
  c) frímerki
  d) pakki

6) clerk
  a) svar
  b) flugpóstur
  c) afgreiðslumaður
  d) heimilisfang

7) export
  a) útfluttningur
  b) að deila
  c) heimilisfang
  d) boðberi

8) airmail
  a) útfluttningur
  b) peningasending
  c) frímerki
  d) flugpóstur

9) post
  a) póstur
  b) flugpóstur
  c) bréfberi
  d) bréf

10) reply
  a) sendandi
  b) heimilisfang
  c) pakki
  d) svar

Word Quiz #144 - Postal

Choose the best Icelandic word to match the English word.

1) package
  a) bréf
  b) innflutningur
  c) pakki
  d) póstur

2) postage stamp
  a) póstbox
  b) frímerki
  c) umslag
  d) peningasending

3) import
  a) bréfberi
  b) bréf
  c) innflutningur
  d) flugpóstur

4) sender
  a) sendandi
  b) pakki
  c) skráð bréf
  d) flugpóstur

5) printed item
  a) að senda
  b) útfluttningur
  c) póstur
  d) prentað bréf

6) airmail
  a) flugpóstur
  b) prentað bréf
  c) innflutningur
  d) að senda

7) to send
  a) flugpóstur
  b) umslag
  c) afgreiðslumaður
  d) að senda

8) to write
  a) útfluttningur
  b) að skrifa
  c) pakki
  d) heimilisfang

9) money order
  a) peningasending
  b) heimilisfang
  c) bréf
  d) frímerki

10) post
  a) flugpóstur
  b) pósthús
  c) póstur
  d) afgreiðslumaður

Word Quiz #145 - Postal

Choose the best Icelandic word to match the English word.

1) reply
 a) peningasending
 b) skráð bréf
 c) svar
 d) að skrifa

2) import
 a) innflutningur
 b) afgreiðslumaður
 c) peningasending
 d) sendandi

3) printed item
 a) svar
 b) umslag
 c) póstbox
 d) prentað bréf

4) money order
 a) peningasending
 b) bréfberi
 c) að skrifa
 d) afgreiðslumaður

5) export
 a) útfluttningur
 b) að deila
 c) prentað bréf
 d) að senda

6) airmail
 a) flugpóstur
 b) boðberi
 c) svar
 d) að skrifa

7) package
 a) boðberi
 b) frímerki
 c) pakki
 d) afgreiðslumaður

8) envelope
 a) bréf
 b) flugpóstur
 c) umslag
 d) að skrifa

9) clerk
 a) afgreiðslumaður
 b) sendandi
 c) innflutningur
 d) að skrifa

10) post
 a) bréfberi
 b) bréf
 c) póstur
 d) að bíða

Word Quiz #146 - Postal

Choose the best Icelandic word to match the English word.

1) registered letter
  a) skráð bréf
  b) bréf
  c) innflutningur
  d) að deila

2) note
  a) að bíða
  b) peningasending
  c) bréf
  d) pósthús

3) address
  a) boðberi
  b) póstur
  c) heimilisfang
  d) póstbox

4) money order
  a) bréf
  b) svar
  c) peningasending
  d) pakki

5) to write
  a) bréf
  b) að skrifa
  c) heimilisfang
  d) umslag

6) to post
  a) peningasending
  b) frímerki
  c) sendandi
  d) að deila

7) printed item
  a) svar
  b) heimilisfang
  c) umslag
  d) prentað bréf

8) post office
  a) póstbox
  b) pakki
  c) bréf
  d) pósthús

9) airmail
  a) frímerki
  b) flugpóstur
  c) bréf
  d) svar

10) sender
  a) að senda
  b) boðberi
  c) útfluttningur
  d) sendandi

Word Quiz #147 - Postal

Choose the best Icelandic word to match the English word.

1) to send
   a) umslag
   b) að senda
   c) prentað bréf
   d) bréfberi

2) reply
   a) póstbox
   b) pósthús
   c) svar
   d) að senda

3) clerk
   a) útfluttningur
   b) peningasending
   c) afgreiðslumaður
   d) sendandi

4) registered letter
   a) bréf
   b) skráð bréf
   c) heimilisfang
   d) að senda

5) postage stamp
   a) umslag
   b) að skrifa
   c) prentað bréf
   d) frímerki

6) import
   a) peningasending
   b) innflutningur
   c) svar
   d) skráð bréf

7) address
   a) afgreiðslumaður
   b) að skrifa
   c) heimilisfang
   d) prentað bréf

8) post
   a) útfluttningur
   b) póstur
   c) að deila
   d) bréf

9) postman
   a) bréfberi
   b) skráð bréf
   c) svar
   d) innflutningur

10) airmail
   a) heimilisfang
   b) flugpóstur
   c) sendandi
   d) að bíða

Word Quiz #148 - Postal

Choose the best Icelandic word to match the English word.

1) import
   a) útfluttningur
   b) póstur
   c) innflutningur
   d) bréfberi

2) postman
   a) bréfberi
   b) bréf
   c) umslag
   d) svar

3) airmail
   a) sendandi
   b) póstbox
   c) prentað bréf
   d) flugpóstur

4) note
   a) sendandi
   b) að skrifa
   c) svar
   d) bréf

5) postage stamp
   a) frímerki
   b) umslag
   c) að senda
   d) svar

6) to post
   a) prentað bréf
   b) frímerki
   c) að deila
   d) að bíða

7) reply
   a) útfluttningur
   b) boðberi
   c) svar
   d) að bíða

8) clerk
   a) sendandi
   b) póstur
   c) prentað bréf
   d) afgreiðslumaður

9) letter
   a) prentað bréf
   b) bréfberi
   c) bréf
   d) frímerki

10) sender
   a) sendandi
   b) heimilisfang
   c) að skrifa
   d) bréf

Word Quiz #149 - Postal

Choose the best Icelandic word to match the English word.

1) to wait
- a) bréfberi
- b) skráð bréf
- c) að bíða
- d) umslag

2) postage stamp
- a) að senda
- b) frímerki
- c) sendandi
- d) að deila

3) letter
- a) boðberi
- b) bréf
- c) póstur
- d) peningasending

4) import
- a) að senda
- b) skráð bréf
- c) útfluttningur
- d) innflutningur

5) postman
- a) bréfberi
- b) boðberi
- c) að skrifa
- d) póstbox

6) to send
- a) að bíða
- b) að senda
- c) prentað bréf
- d) útfluttningur

7) money order
- a) að senda
- b) peningasending
- c) boðberi
- d) að bíða

8) package
- a) pakki
- b) bréfberi
- c) að bíða
- d) prentað bréf

9) clerk
- a) afgreiðslumaður
- b) peningasending
- c) póstur
- d) skráð bréf

10) registered letter
- a) skráð bréf
- b) að senda
- c) peningasending
- d) að skrifa

Word Quiz #150 - Postal

Choose the best Icelandic word to match the English word.

1) address
 a) skráð bréf
 b) bréfberi
 c) að deila
 d) heimilisfang

2) letterbox
 a) svar
 b) pósthús
 c) póstbox
 d) frímerki

3) import
 a) peningasending
 b) bréf
 c) innflutningur
 d) svar

4) post office
 a) pakki
 b) að deila
 c) pósthús
 d) afgreiðslumaður

5) export
 a) flugpóstur
 b) að senda
 c) heimilisfang
 d) útfluttningur

6) to send
 a) að senda
 b) að deila
 c) sendandi
 d) svar

7) reply
 a) heimilisfang
 b) póstur
 c) póstbox
 d) svar

8) airmail
 a) að skrifa
 b) heimilisfang
 c) flugpóstur
 d) peningasending

9) post
 a) boðberi
 b) frímerki
 c) að bíða
 d) póstur

10) note
 a) prentað bréf
 b) sendandi
 c) að skrifa
 d) bréf

Word Quiz #151 - Sightseeing

Choose the best English word to match the Icelandic word.

1) sjór
- a) sea
- b) field
- c) plain
- d) rock

2) frumskógur
- a) cape
- b) ocean
- c) atmosphere
- d) jungle

3) mýri
- a) river
- b) beach
- c) marsh
- d) mountain

4) umhverfi
- a) environment
- b) dam
- c) meadow
- d) countryside

5) fjörður
- a) mountain
- b) bay
- c) cave
- d) earthquake

6) sjávarföll
- a) marsh
- b) river
- c) coast
- d) tide

7) strönd
- a) grass
- b) plain
- c) countryside
- d) beach

8) hellir
- a) stone
- b) cave
- c) meadow
- d) island

9) gjá
- a) river
- b) meadow
- c) gulf
- d) desert

10) stífla
- a) ocean
- b) dam
- c) pond
- d) environment

Word Quiz #152 - Sightseeing

Choose the best English word to match the Icelandic word.

1) akur
- a) river
- b) coast
- c) sea
- d) field

2) fjall
- a) canal
- b) mountain
- c) cave
- d) bay

3) sjávarföll
- a) dam
- b) island
- c) tide
- d) field

4) skógur
- a) pond
- b) tide
- c) grass
- d) forest

5) sjávarströnd
- a) atmosphere
- b) coast
- c) rock
- d) lake

6) andrúmsloft
- a) lake
- b) mountain
- c) atmosphere
- d) plain

7) flatlendi
- a) plain
- b) island
- c) mountain
- d) river

8) engi
- a) forest
- b) meadow
- c) rock
- d) earthquake

9) fjörður
- a) bay
- b) river
- c) cape
- d) sand

10) eyja
- a) hill
- b) sea
- c) marsh
- d) island

Word Quiz #153 - Sightseeing

Choose the best English word to match the Icelandic word.

1) sandur
   a) beach
   b) coast
   c) sand
   d) rock

2) fjall
   a) gulf
   b) nature
   c) mountain
   d) atmosphere

3) landslag
   a) cape
   b) forest
   c) landscape
   d) gulf

4) stífla
   a) gulf
   b) environment
   c) dam
   d) stone

5) skurður
   a) pond
   b) meadow
   c) canal
   d) plain

6) engi
   a) meadow
   b) earthquake
   c) dam
   d) sand

7) frumskógur
   a) mountain
   b) gulf
   c) plain
   d) jungle

8) skógur
   a) rock
   b) forest
   c) field
   d) earthquake

9) nes
   a) grass
   b) bay
   c) cave
   d) cape

10) umhverfi
   a) field
   b) pond
   c) environment
   d) nature

Word Quiz #154 - Sightseeing

Choose the best English word to match the Icelandic word.

1) eyðimörk
   a) desert
   b) coast
   c) environment
   d) stone

2) sjávarföll
   a) grass
   b) island
   c) tide
   d) forest

3) skagi
   a) cave
   b) plain
   c) peninsula
   d) field

4) stífla
   a) rock
   b) grass
   c) environment
   d) dam

5) fjall
   a) hill
   b) sea
   c) mountain
   d) island

6) sjór
   a) sea
   b) atmosphere
   c) mountain
   d) beach

7) skurður
   a) canal
   b) bay
   c) countryside
   d) island

8) steinn
   a) stone
   b) sand
   c) gulf
   d) tide

9) sjávarströnd
   a) coast
   b) mountain
   c) stone
   d) sea

10) gjá
   a) cave
   b) gulf
   c) plain
   d) lake

Word Quiz #155 - Sightseeing

Choose the best English word to match the Icelandic word.

1) stífla
   a) dam
   b) island
   c) cave
   d) earthquake

2) jarðskjálfti
   a) lake
   b) earthquake
   c) stone
   d) cave

3) fjörður
   a) beach
   b) bay
   c) atmosphere
   d) desert

4) nes
   a) cape
   b) forest
   c) jungle
   d) cave

5) andrúmsloft
   a) mountain
   b) atmosphere
   c) jungle
   d) lake

6) sandur
   a) nature
   b) field
   c) rock
   d) sand

7) eyja
   a) earthquake
   b) rock
   c) island
   d) stone

8) steinn
   a) forest
   b) mountain
   c) stone
   d) sand

9) eyðimörk
   a) desert
   b) landscape
   c) pond
   d) rock

10) á
   a) nature
   b) river
   c) earthquake
   d) cave

Word Quiz #156 - Sightseeing

Choose the best English word to match the Icelandic word.

1) náttúra
   a) peninsula
   b) stone
   c) gulf
   d) nature

2) skagi
   a) coast
   b) peninsula
   c) environment
   d) forest

3) sjór
   a) desert
   b) sea
   c) coast
   d) lake

4) gras
   a) grass
   b) tide
   c) meadow
   d) atmosphere

5) gjá
   a) beach
   b) gulf
   c) coast
   d) desert

6) stífla
   a) dam
   b) landscape
   c) bay
   d) tide

7) sandur
   a) nature
   b) sand
   c) atmosphere
   d) pond

8) flatlendi
   a) sand
   b) plain
   c) beach
   d) river

9) fjörður
   a) meadow
   b) desert
   c) bay
   d) river

10) steinn
   a) stone
   b) grass
   c) beach
   d) river

Word Quiz #157 - Sightseeing

Choose the best English word to match the Icelandic word.

1) steinn
   a) meadow
   b) jungle
   c) island
   d) stone

2) fjall
   a) earthquake
   b) peninsula
   c) mountain
   d) lake

3) gjá
   a) mountain
   b) gulf
   c) atmosphere
   d) nature

4) mýri
   a) landscape
   b) field
   c) marsh
   d) sand

5) fjörður
   a) grass
   b) nature
   c) bay
   d) environment

6) sjávarströnd
   a) island
   b) rock
   c) beach
   d) coast

7) flatlendi
   a) plain
   b) bay
   c) lake
   d) grass

8) frumskógur
   a) environment
   b) jungle
   c) river
   d) hill

9) sjór
   a) sea
   b) atmosphere
   c) nature
   d) hill

10) sandur
   a) sand
   b) forest
   c) lake
   d) sea

Word Quiz #158 - Sightseeing

Choose the best English word to match the Icelandic word.

1) steinn
a) sand
b) gulf
c) stone
d) landscape

2) skagi
a) hill
b) bay
c) peninsula
d) earthquake

3) nes
a) environment
b) jungle
c) cape
d) rock

4) jarðskjálfti
a) lake
b) dam
c) earthquake
d) atmosphere

5) sjávarströnd
a) hill
b) nature
c) sand
d) coast

6) gras
a) stone
b) sand
c) cave
d) grass

7) strönd
a) tide
b) earthquake
c) beach
d) atmosphere

8) náttúra
a) nature
b) tide
c) coast
d) ocean

9) skurður
a) plain
b) dam
c) canal
d) peninsula

10) akur
a) gulf
b) meadow
c) field
d) earthquake

Word Quiz #159 - Sightseeing

Choose the best English word to match the Icelandic word.

1) steinn
   a) tide
   b) desert
   c) stone
   d) sea

2) skógur
   a) meadow
   b) field
   c) forest
   d) hill

3) stífla
   a) atmosphere
   b) dam
   c) plain
   d) sea

4) frumskógur
   a) nature
   b) island
   c) jungle
   d) meadow

5) fjörður
   a) jungle
   b) bay
   c) pond
   d) grass

6) steinn
   a) rock
   b) lake
   c) earthquake
   d) sand

7) mýri
   a) coast
   b) mountain
   c) marsh
   d) field

8) skagi
   a) peninsula
   b) sand
   c) earthquake
   d) pond

9) umhverfi
   a) grass
   b) rock
   c) gulf
   d) environment

10) jarðskjálfti
   a) island
   b) earthquake
   c) forest
   d) countryside

Word Quiz #160 - Sightseeing

Choose the best English word to match the Icelandic word.

1) steinn
  a) rock
  b) gulf
  c) hill
  d) dam

2) sandur
  a) beach
  b) sand
  c) field
  d) countryside

3) akur
  a) field
  b) sand
  c) landscape
  d) marsh

4) skógur
  a) meadow
  b) forest
  c) desert
  d) countryside

5) sjór
  a) sea
  b) jungle
  c) marsh
  d) hill

6) sjávarströnd
  a) sea
  b) cape
  c) coast
  d) environment

7) flatlendi
  a) beach
  b) plain
  c) field
  d) sea

8) mýri
  a) bay
  b) canal
  c) marsh
  d) jungle

9) engi
  a) mountain
  b) meadow
  c) grass
  d) marsh

10) eyðimörk
  a) forest
  b) desert
  c) dam
  d) earthquake

Word Quiz #161 - Sightseeing

Choose the best English word to match the Icelandic word.

1) landslag
  a) dam
  b) landscape
  c) marsh
  d) sand

2) fjörður
  a) bay
  b) grass
  c) earthquake
  d) desert

3) eyðimörk
  a) field
  b) desert
  c) beach
  d) coast

4) á
  a) gulf
  b) coast
  c) nature
  d) river

5) hellir
  a) cave
  b) landscape
  c) desert
  d) ocean

6) sjávarströnd
  a) bay
  b) countryside
  c) canal
  d) coast

7) haf
  a) environment
  b) rock
  c) meadow
  d) ocean

8) fjall
  a) lake
  b) grass
  c) tide
  d) mountain

9) hæð
  a) hill
  b) plain
  c) desert
  d) field

10) lækur
  a) nature
  b) hill
  c) forest
  d) lake

Word Quiz #162 - Sightseeing

Choose the best English word to match the Icelandic word.

1) sjór
   a) plain
   b) jungle
   c) field
   d) sea

2) skagi
   a) earthquake
   b) peninsula
   c) field
   d) river

3) stífla
   a) field
   b) sand
   c) desert
   d) dam

4) mýri
   a) bay
   b) marsh
   c) meadow
   d) stone

5) sandur
   a) ocean
   b) countryside
   c) forest
   d) sand

6) frumskógur
   a) jungle
   b) coast
   c) earthquake
   d) mountain

7) skógur
   a) nature
   b) beach
   c) forest
   d) ocean

8) engi
   a) pond
   b) meadow
   c) bay
   d) nature

9) jarðskjálfti
   a) field
   b) earthquake
   c) mountain
   d) desert

10) gjá
   a) dam
   b) mountain
   c) environment
   d) gulf

Word Quiz #163 - Sightseeing

Choose the best English word to match the Icelandic word.

1) skagi
 a) peninsula
 b) atmosphere
 c) earthquake
 d) gulf

2) haf
 a) countryside
 b) environment
 c) ocean
 d) island

3) flatlendi
 a) plain
 b) desert
 c) atmosphere
 d) cave

4) hæð
 a) hill
 b) marsh
 c) tide
 d) forest

5) sjávarföll
 a) nature
 b) dam
 c) tide
 d) bay

6) skurður
 a) canal
 b) gulf
 c) meadow
 d) rock

7) stífla
 a) canal
 b) lake
 c) dam
 d) cape

8) umhverfi
 a) sea
 b) atmosphere
 c) desert
 d) environment

9) tjörn
 a) pond
 b) grass
 c) field
 d) forest

10) engi
 a) grass
 b) hill
 c) countryside
 d) meadow

Word Quiz #164 - Sightseeing

Choose the best Icelandic word to match the English word.

1) grass
   a) skógur
   b) gras
   c) skurður
   d) sandur

2) jungle
   a) frumskógur
   b) eyja
   c) haf
   d) steinn

3) coast
   a) sjávarströnd
   b) frumskógur
   c) umhverfi
   d) nes

4) bay
   a) hellir
   b) haf
   c) flatlendi
   d) fjörður

5) hill
   a) hæð
   b) steinn
   c) lækur
   d) akur

6) gulf
   a) gjá
   b) steinn
   c) eyja
   d) skagi

7) cave
   a) akur
   b) hellir
   c) frumskógur
   d) eyðimörk

8) forest
   a) tjörn
   b) skógur
   c) gras
   d) umhverfi

9) ocean
   a) sjór
   b) haf
   c) skurður
   d) nes

10) plain
   a) á
   b) fjall
   c) landslag
   d) flatlendi

Word Quiz #165 - Sightseeing

Choose the best Icelandic word to match the English word.

1) forest
a) náttúra
b) gras
c) skógur
d) frumskógur

2) ocean
a) haf
b) frumskógur
c) landslag
d) sandur

3) field
a) gras
b) sjávarströnd
c) sjór
d) akur

4) gulf
a) gjá
b) sandur
c) skógur
d) landslag

5) lake
a) á
b) lækur
c) skógur
d) skagi

6) plain
a) flatlendi
b) haf
c) skógur
d) sjávarföll

7) rock
a) andrúmsloft
b) sjór
c) steinn
d) sjávarströnd

8) meadow
a) engi
b) hæð
c) eyðimörk
d) tjörn

9) jungle
a) nes
b) sveit
c) frumskógur
d) gras

10) stone
a) sjávarföll
b) strönd
c) hellir
d) steinn

Word Quiz #166 - Sightseeing

Choose the best Icelandic word to match the English word.

1) bay
a) landslag
b) haf
c) fjörður
d) hæð

2) nature
a) haf
b) nes
c) náttúra
d) hæð

3) peninsula
a) skógur
b) skagi
c) fjall
d) stífla

4) rock
a) eyja
b) sjór
c) steinn
d) stífla

5) beach
a) andrúmsloft
b) fjall
c) strönd
d) skurður

6) pond
a) engi
b) tjörn
c) akur
d) sjór

7) island
a) flatlendi
b) eyja
c) skurður
d) gras

8) tide
a) andrúmsloft
b) eyja
c) sjávarströnd
d) sjávarföll

9) sand
a) akur
b) eyja
c) gras
d) sandur

10) marsh
a) andrúmsloft
b) mýri
c) skurður
d) skógur

Word Quiz #167 - Sightseeing

Choose the best Icelandic word to match the English word.

1) grass
   a) gras
   b) jarðskjálfti
   c) fjall
   d) strönd

2) dam
   a) stífla
   b) sjávarströnd
   c) lækur
   d) skurður

3) bay
   a) jarðskjálfti
   b) fjörður
   c) sjávarströnd
   d) lækur

4) hill
   a) hæð
   b) náttúra
   c) sjávarströnd
   d) fjall

5) sea
   a) sandur
   b) sjór
   c) andrúmsloft
   d) gras

6) desert
   a) skagi
   b) sjávarströnd
   c) eyðimörk
   d) skurður

7) meadow
   a) hellir
   b) fjall
   c) engi
   d) náttúra

8) countryside
   a) sjór
   b) sveit
   c) fjall
   d) sjávarströnd

9) landscape
   a) gras
   b) landslag
   c) akur
   d) hellir

10) mountain
   a) fjall
   b) steinn
   c) strönd
   d) hæð

Word Quiz #168 - Sightseeing
Choose the best Icelandic word to match the English word.

1) jungle
a) á
b) sjór
c) steinn
d) frumskógur

2) stone
a) lækur
b) steinn
c) skagi
d) fjörður

3) canal
a) engi
b) skurður
c) flatlendi
d) jarðskjálfti

4) dam
a) stífla
b) á
c) landslag
d) jarðskjálfti

5) cave
a) eyðimörk
b) hellir
c) haf
d) nes

6) rock
a) skógur
b) sandur
c) andrúmsloft
d) steinn

7) sand
a) nes
b) sjór
c) sandur
d) flatlendi

8) coast
a) sjór
b) sjávarströnd
c) strönd
d) stífla

9) grass
a) fjall
b) gras
c) landslag
d) sandur

10) countryside
a) sjór
b) sveit
c) lækur
d) akur

Word Quiz #169 - Sightseeing

Choose the best Icelandic word to match the English word.

1) gulf
 a) gjá
 b) sjávarströnd
 c) eyja
 d) skógur

2) bay
 a) andrúmsloft
 b) sjávarföll
 c) eyja
 d) fjörður

3) plain
 a) flatlendi
 b) akur
 c) andrúmsloft
 d) sjór

4) atmosphere
 a) andrúmsloft
 b) hellir
 c) mýri
 d) sjávarföll

5) sand
 a) sjávarströnd
 b) sandur
 c) steinn
 d) gras

6) rock
 a) steinn
 b) stífla
 c) náttúra
 d) flatlendi

7) tide
 a) haf
 b) sandur
 c) sjávarföll
 d) skógur

8) pond
 a) tjörn
 b) haf
 c) náttúra
 d) frumskógur

9) island
 a) strönd
 b) gras
 c) eyja
 d) haf

10) sea
 a) náttúra
 b) gjá
 c) landslag
 d) sjór

Word Quiz #170 - Sightseeing

Choose the best Icelandic word to match the English word.

1) atmosphere
- a) hellir
- b) steinn
- c) eyja
- d) andrúmsloft

2) island
- a) eyja
- b) tjörn
- c) náttúra
- d) landslag

3) field
- a) hellir
- b) tjörn
- c) akur
- d) flatlendi

4) mountain
- a) fjall
- b) sandur
- c) skógur
- d) gras

5) marsh
- a) sjór
- b) flatlendi
- c) umhverfi
- d) mýri

6) meadow
- a) mýri
- b) engi
- c) landslag
- d) haf

7) pond
- a) skurður
- b) strönd
- c) fjall
- d) tjörn

8) dam
- a) frumskógur
- b) stífla
- c) eyja
- d) landslag

9) landscape
- a) akur
- b) landslag
- c) skógur
- d) sjór

10) grass
- a) sveit
- b) eyja
- c) gras
- d) mýri

Word Quiz #171 - Sightseeing

Choose the best Icelandic word to match the English word.

1) hill
   a) andrúmsloft
   b) hæð
   c) fjall
   d) sjávarföll

2) tide
   a) sjávarföll
   b) lækur
   c) skagi
   d) nes

3) desert
   a) landslag
   b) náttúra
   c) eyðimörk
   d) nes

4) environment
   a) frumskógur
   b) umhverfi
   c) skógur
   d) skagi

5) lake
   a) nes
   b) náttúra
   c) lækur
   d) skurður

6) atmosphere
   a) á
   b) eyðimörk
   c) andrúmsloft
   d) fjall

7) landscape
   a) landslag
   b) steinn
   c) akur
   d) haf

8) forest
   a) jarðskjálfti
   b) skógur
   c) sjávarföll
   d) engi

9) ocean
   a) sjávarföll
   b) haf
   c) á
   d) hæð

10) pond
   a) tjörn
   b) steinn
   c) umhverfi
   d) andrúmsloft

Word Quiz #172 - Sightseeing

Choose the best Icelandic word to match the English word.

1) earthquake
- a) gjá
- b) jarðskjálfti
- c) hellir
- d) stífla

2) countryside
- a) stífla
- b) steinn
- c) sveit
- d) sjávarföll

3) marsh
- a) eyja
- b) hellir
- c) mýri
- d) nes

4) bay
- a) strönd
- b) gjá
- c) fjörður
- d) umhverfi

5) cave
- a) hellir
- b) steinn
- c) skógur
- d) eyðimörk

6) beach
- a) skógur
- b) eyja
- c) strönd
- d) sandur

7) pond
- a) skógur
- b) tjörn
- c) sjávarströnd
- d) eyðimörk

8) sand
- a) sjór
- b) eyðimörk
- c) sandur
- d) flatlendi

9) gulf
- a) gjá
- b) sveit
- c) sjór
- d) haf

10) plain
- a) flatlendi
- b) tjörn
- c) eyðimörk
- d) lækur

Word Quiz #173 - Sightseeing

Choose the best Icelandic word to match the English word.

1) environment
- a) landslag
- b) eyja
- c) umhverfi
- d) nes

2) nature
- a) náttúra
- b) haf
- c) á
- d) sjávarströnd

3) sea
- a) frumskógur
- b) steinn
- c) flatlendi
- d) sjór

4) atmosphere
- a) haf
- b) skurður
- c) andrúmsloft
- d) skagi

5) island
- a) haf
- b) landslag
- c) andrúmsloft
- d) eyja

6) bay
- a) skógur
- b) haf
- c) gjá
- d) fjörður

7) canal
- a) tjörn
- b) skurður
- c) náttúra
- d) akur

8) landscape
- a) flatlendi
- b) sveit
- c) landslag
- d) á

9) dam
- a) stífla
- b) skagi
- c) sjávarföll
- d) frumskógur

10) mountain
- a) fjall
- b) skurður
- c) steinn
- d) lækur

Word Quiz #174 - Sightseeing

Choose the best Icelandic word to match the English word.

1) canal
 a) skurður
 b) sveit
 c) á
 d) landslag

2) atmosphere
 a) steinn
 b) skurður
 c) andrúmsloft
 d) gras

3) island
 a) náttúra
 b) skógur
 c) gras
 d) eyja

4) marsh
 a) sveit
 b) mýri
 c) flatlendi
 d) frumskógur

5) countryside
 a) gjá
 b) sveit
 c) hæð
 d) skurður

6) river
 a) nes
 b) gras
 c) sjávarföll
 d) á

7) sea
 a) haf
 b) skagi
 c) sjór
 d) stífla

8) lake
 a) hæð
 b) sjávarströnd
 c) lækur
 d) engi

9) landscape
 a) lækur
 b) fjall
 c) steinn
 d) landslag

10) coast
 a) sjávarföll
 b) sjávarströnd
 c) gras
 d) eyðimörk

Word Quiz #175 - Sightseeing

Choose the best Icelandic word to match the English word.

1) island
- a) landslag
- b) steinn
- c) eyja
- d) sveit

2) cave
- a) sjávarföll
- b) steinn
- c) á
- d) hellir

3) meadow
- a) skógur
- b) akur
- c) mýri
- d) engi

4) river
- a) landslag
- b) á
- c) lækur
- d) flatlendi

5) hill
- a) tjörn
- b) sjór
- c) hæð
- d) lækur

6) coast
- a) gjá
- b) fjall
- c) sjávarströnd
- d) andrúmsloft

7) field
- a) akur
- b) fjall
- c) jarðskjálfti
- d) sjávarföll

8) rock
- a) sjávarströnd
- b) eyðimörk
- c) steinn
- d) á

9) bay
- a) jarðskjálfti
- b) fjörður
- c) eyja
- d) sjávarströnd

10) stone
- a) náttúra
- b) steinn
- c) sjór
- d) akur

Word Quiz #176 - Zoo

Choose the best English word to match the Icelandic word.

1) jurtaæta
- a) herbivore
- b) zoo
- c) panther
- d) baboon

2) hlébarði
- a) zoo visitor
- b) giraffe house
- c) leopard
- d) reptile enclosure

3) refur
- a) dangerous
- b) aquarium
- c) fox
- d) aquatic

4) gíraffahús
- a) jaguar
- b) glass case
- c) cougar
- d) giraffe house

5) fjallaljón
- a) cougar
- b) monkey
- c) elephant
- d) zebra

6) nashyrningur
- a) giraffe
- b) zoo
- c) rhinoceros
- d) vertebrate

7) bavían
- a) baboon
- b) poisonous
- c) hyena
- d) leopard

8) dýr
- a) glass case
- b) lion
- c) amphibian
- d) animal

9) mammaldýr
- a) panda
- b) nocturnal
- c) bear
- d) aardvark

10) froskdýr
- a) amphibian
- b) baboon
- c) zoo
- d) crocodile

Word Quiz #177 - Zoo

Choose the best English word to match the Icelandic word.

1) fílagirðing
   a) koala
   b) elephant enclosure
   c) crocodile
   d) aquarium

2) jarðneskur
   a) alligator
   b) reptile enclosure
   c) terrestrial
   d) zookeeper

3) utandyra girðing
   a) amphibian
   b) outdoor enclosure
   c) carnivore
   d) monkey

4) ljón
   a) reptile
   b) aquatic
   c) lion
   d) monkey house

5) tegundir
   a) species
   b) giraffe house
   c) zoo visitor
   d) anteater

6) skriðdýr
   a) giraffe
   b) reptile
   c) nocturnal
   d) admission

7) fíll
   a) leopard
   b) animal
   c) elephant
   d) monkey

8) fuglasafn
   a) kangaroo
   b) amphibian
   c) enclosing wall
   d) aviary

9) utandyra búr
   a) leopard
   b) dangerous
   c) hyena
   d) outside cage

10) krókódíll
   a) zookeeper
   b) aviary
   c) crocodile
   d) hippopotamus

Word Quiz #178 - Zoo

Choose the best English word to match the Icelandic word.

1) flóðhestur
a) kangaroo
b) fox
c) anteater
d) hippopotamus

2) fíll
a) elephant
b) aardvark
c) terrestrial
d) jaguar

3) hryggleysingjar
a) fierce
b) reptile
c) vertebrate
d) monkey

4) björn
a) reptile enclosure
b) bear
c) outside cage
d) vertebrate

5) hjörtur
a) gazelle
b) anteater
c) enclosing wall
d) zoo

6) næturdýr
a) diurnal
b) zebra
c) nocturnal
d) anteater

7) utandyra búr
a) jaguar
b) outside cage
c) aviary
d) baboon

8) gorilla
a) leopard
b) species
c) gorilla
d) vertebrate

9) refur
a) fox
b) outside cage
c) mammal
d) zebra

10) aðgangur
a) glass case
b) cougar
c) admission
d) terrestrial

Word Quiz #179 - Zoo

Choose the best English word to match the Icelandic word.

1) skriðdýr
a) panther
b) amphibian
c) reptile
d) alligator

2) dýragarðsvörður
a) zookeeper
b) glass case
c) species
d) cheetah

3) fílahús
a) poisonous
b) glass case
c) elephant house
d) vertebrate

4) krókódíll
a) crocodile
b) enclosing wall
c) outside cage
d) tiger

5) pardusdýr
a) aardvark
b) alligator
c) panther
d) hippopotamus

6) kóalabjörn
a) dangerous
b) panther
c) diurnal
d) koala

7) sebrahestur
a) enclosing wall
b) baboon
c) rhinoceros
d) zebra

8) blettatígur
a) mammal
b) cheetah
c) terrestrial
d) wolf

9) ljón
a) hyena
b) elephant enclosure
c) mammal
d) lion

10) kengúra
a) terrestrial
b) kangaroo
c) gorilla
d) elephant enclosure

Word Quiz #180 - Zoo

Choose the best English word to match the Icelandic word.

1) api
  a) reptile enclosure
  b) alligator
  c) aquatic
  d) monkey

2) rándýr
  a) carnivore
  b) jaguar
  c) elephant enclosure
  d) zookeeper

3) skriðdýragirðing
  a) giraffe house
  b) reptile enclosure
  c) hyena
  d) rhinoceros

4) gíraffi
  a) giraffe
  b) dangerous
  c) reptile enclosure
  d) zoo

5) sædýr
  a) tiger
  b) aquatic
  c) cheetah
  d) fierce

6) panda
  a) panda
  b) monkey
  c) aquatic
  d) leopard

7) hlébarði
  a) elephant
  b) monkey
  c) koala
  d) leopard

8) dýr
  a) crocodile
  b) hyena
  c) enclosing wall
  d) animal

9) hyena
  a) hyena
  b) aardvark
  c) zoo
  d) gazelle

10) utandyra búr
  a) outside cage
  b) tiger
  c) jaguar
  d) gorilla

Word Quiz #181 - Zoo

Choose the best English word to match the Icelandic word.

1) skriðdýragirðing
   a) elephant
   b) cheetah
   c) elephant house
   d) reptile enclosure

2) sædýrabúr
   a) aquarium
   b) panther
   c) aquatic
   d) reptile enclosure

3) girðing
   a) alligator
   b) crocodile
   c) gazelle
   d) enclosing wall

4) gíraffi
   a) dangerous
   b) aardvark
   c) giraffe
   d) monkey house

5) hryggleysingjar
   a) vertebrate
   b) zoo
   c) outdoor enclosure
   d) armadillo

6) ljón
   a) gorilla
   b) lion
   c) vertebrate
   d) elephant

7) refur
   a) arboreal
   b) panda
   c) admission
   d) fox

8) sebrahestur
   a) animal
   b) rhinoceros
   c) zebra
   d) zoo

9) jaguar
   a) zebra
   b) jaguar
   c) rhinoceros
   d) panther

10) krókódíll
   a) outdoor enclosure
   b) baboon
   c) jaguar
   d) crocodile

Word Quiz #182 - Zoo

Choose the best English word to match the Icelandic word.

1) gíraffi
a) giraffe
b) zoo
c) aquatic
d) amphibian

2) krókódíll
a) alligator
b) kangaroo
c) zoo visitor
d) monkey house

3) gíraffahús
a) alligator
b) rhinoceros
c) monkey house
d) giraffe house

4) hjörtur
a) gazelle
b) dangerous
c) elephant house
d) giraffe house

5) fuglasafn
a) reptile enclosure
b) tiger
c) aviary
d) zoo visitor

6) panda
a) elephant enclosure
b) species
c) panda
d) terrestrial

7) kengúra
a) fox
b) hippopotamus
c) kangaroo
d) outside cage

8) mamaldýr
a) baboon
b) reptile enclosure
c) enclosing wall
d) mammal

9) aðgangur
a) admission
b) elephant enclosure
c) poisonous
d) elephant

10) api
a) monkey
b) species
c) fierce
d) enclosing wall

Word Quiz #183 - Zoo

Choose the best English word to match the Icelandic word.

1) fílagirðing
a) nocturnal
b) elephant enclosure
c) crocodile
d) armadillo

2) fíll
a) aardvark
b) zoo
c) tiger
d) elephant

3) rándýr
a) glass case
b) zoo
c) carnivore
d) zookeeper

4) hættulegur
a) dangerous
b) tiger
c) aquatic
d) lion

5) nashyrningur
a) amphibian
b) outside cage
c) rhinoceros
d) kangaroo

6) kengúra
a) kangaroo
b) koala
c) nocturnal
d) aquarium

7) úlfur
a) wolf
b) crocodile
c) cheetah
d) species

8) girðing
a) aviary
b) terrestrial
c) enclosing wall
d) gazelle

9) fjallaljón
a) glass case
b) zebra
c) cougar
d) hippopotamus

10) mammaldýr
a) glass case
b) panda
c) aardvark
d) aviary

Word Quiz #184 - Zoo
Choose the best English word to match the Icelandic word.

1) gorilla
    a) bear
    b) gorilla
    c) cheetah
    d) glass case

2) dýr
    a) mammal
    b) animal
    c) leopard
    d) arboreal

3) girðing
    a) enclosing wall
    b) cheetah
    c) vertebrate
    d) arboreal

4) beltisdýr
    a) giraffe
    b) glass case
    c) armadillo
    d) elephant enclosure

5) hyena
    a) gorilla
    b) terrestrial
    c) poisonous
    d) hyena

6) utandyra búr
    a) outside cage
    b) animal
    c) admission
    d) aquatic

7) næturdýr
    a) nocturnal
    b) aquarium
    c) koala
    d) diurnal

8) björn
    a) cougar
    b) bear
    c) admission
    d) giraffe house

9) skriðdýr
    a) panther
    b) fox
    c) glass case
    d) reptile

10) hjörtur
    a) alligator
    b) gazelle
    c) elephant enclosure
    d) terrestrial

Word Quiz #185 - Zoo

Choose the best English word to match the Icelandic word.

1) gorilla
   a) terrestrial
   b) gorilla
   c) diurnal
   d) glass case

2) panda
   a) admission
   b) panda
   c) herbivore
   d) monkey house

3) hlébarði
   a) reptile
   b) panther
   c) monkey house
   d) leopard

4) beltisdýr
   a) wolf
   b) armadillo
   c) reptile
   d) monkey house

5) hryggleysingjar
   a) crocodile
   b) reptile
   c) amphibian
   d) vertebrate

6) næturdýr
   a) baboon
   b) nocturnal
   c) zookeeper
   d) zoo

7) hættulegur
   a) lion
   b) dangerous
   c) giraffe house
   d) cougar

8) api
   a) rhinoceros
   b) carnivore
   c) monkey
   d) kangaroo

9) refur
   a) kangaroo
   b) animal
   c) giraffe house
   d) fox

10) dagdýr
   a) poisonous
   b) monkey
   c) armadillo
   d) diurnal

Word Quiz #186 - Zoo

Choose the best English word to match the Icelandic word.

1) skriðdýr
   a) giraffe
   b) cougar
   c) reptile
   d) gazelle

2) fjallaljón
   a) cheetah
   b) reptile enclosure
   c) cougar
   d) anteater

3) glerbúr
   a) reptile enclosure
   b) baboon
   c) arboreal
   d) glass case

4) fílahús
   a) leopard
   b) elephant house
   c) baboon
   d) outdoor enclosure

5) dýragarðsvörður
   a) species
   b) kangaroo
   c) leopard
   d) zookeeper

6) hættulegur
   a) zoo visitor
   b) giraffe
   c) enclosing wall
   d) dangerous

7) ljón
   a) giraffe house
   b) lion
   c) zoo
   d) zoo visitor

8) apahús
   a) monkey house
   b) outside cage
   c) nocturnal
   d) giraffe house

9) skriðdýragirðing
   a) fierce
   b) rhinoceros
   c) jaguar
   d) reptile enclosure

10) dýragarður
   a) panther
   b) admission
   c) giraffe
   d) zoo

Word Quiz #187 - Zoo

Choose the best English word to match the Icelandic word.

1) mauraæta
   a) enclosing wall
   b) anteater
   c) nocturnal
   d) koala

2) froskdýr
   a) rhinoceros
   b) amphibian
   c) anteater
   d) giraffe house

3) eitraður
   a) fierce
   b) aviary
   c) reptile
   d) poisonous

4) dýragarðsvörður
   a) kangaroo
   b) alligator
   c) zookeeper
   d) cougar

5) björn
   a) monkey house
   b) crocodile
   c) elephant house
   d) bear

6) ljón
   a) lion
   b) crocodile
   c) anteater
   d) poisonous

7) beltisdýr
   a) tiger
   b) rhinoceros
   c) panda
   d) armadillo

8) aðgangur
   a) zoo visitor
   b) crocodile
   c) admission
   d) poisonous

9) trjábýll
   a) arboreal
   b) monkey house
   c) dangerous
   d) monkey

10) mammaldýr
   a) monkey
   b) aardvark
   c) glass case
   d) hippopotamus

Word Quiz #188 - Zoo

Choose the best English word to match the Icelandic word.

1) jarðneskur
   a) terrestrial
   b) wolf
   c) giraffe
   d) mammal

2) jaguar
   a) species
   b) mammal
   c) jaguar
   d) arboreal

3) tígur
   a) tiger
   b) mammal
   c) aquatic
   d) panther

4) bavían
   a) enclosing wall
   b) anteater
   c) baboon
   d) tiger

5) hyena
   a) gazelle
   b) hyena
   c) tiger
   d) arboreal

6) tegundir
   a) alligator
   b) species
   c) cheetah
   d) reptile enclosure

7) glerbúr
   a) panther
   b) elephant
   c) bear
   d) glass case

8) gíraffahús
   a) aquatic
   b) aardvark
   c) cheetah
   d) giraffe house

9) gorilla
   a) terrestrial
   b) panther
   c) gorilla
   d) diurnal

10) apahús
   a) monkey house
   b) zoo visitor
   c) giraffe
   d) baboon

Word Quiz #189 - Zoo

Choose the best Icelandic word to match the English word.

1) panda
   a) panda
   b) bavían
   c) tígur
   d) sædýrabúr

2) elephant enclosure
   a) mamaldýr
   b) sebrahestur
   c) fílagirðing
   d) apahús

3) zoo
   a) krókódíll
   b) dýragarður
   c) gorilla
   d) trjábýll

4) dangerous
   a) hættulegur
   b) trjábýll
   c) gorilla
   d) apahús

5) lion
   a) jaguar
   b) tígur
   c) næturdýr
   d) ljón

6) bear
   a) úlfur
   b) björn
   c) skriðdýragirðing
   d) mauraæta

7) zookeeper
   a) utandyra búr
   b) jaguar
   c) api
   d) dýragarðsvörður

8) armadillo
   a) trjábýll
   b) bavían
   c) beltisdýr
   d) gíraffahús

9) animal
   a) refur
   b) dýr
   c) fíll
   d) skriðdýr

10) wolf
   a) glerbúr
   b) hættulegur
   c) sebrahestur
   d) úlfur

Word Quiz #190 - Zoo

Choose the best Icelandic word to match the English word.

1) tiger
 a) panda
 b) jurtaæta
 c) fuglasafn
 d) tígur

2) monkey house
 a) dýragarðsgestur
 b) fíll
 c) mamaldýr
 d) apahús

3) gazelle
 a) mamaldýr
 b) hjörtur
 c) fuglasafn
 d) hlébarði

4) elephant house
 a) mamaldýr
 b) hjörtur
 c) kengúra
 d) fílahús

5) elephant enclosure
 a) ljón
 b) fílagirðing
 c) krókódíll
 d) blettatígur

6) fierce
 a) grimmilegur
 b) úlfur
 c) utandyra girðing
 d) skriðdýr

7) bear
 a) dýragarðsvörður
 b) kengúra
 c) björn
 d) hyena

8) arboreal
 a) dýragarðsgestur
 b) trjábýll
 c) api
 d) krókódíll

9) monkey
 a) api
 b) trjábýll
 c) beltisdýr
 d) gorilla

10) zoo visitor
 a) aðgangur
 b) dýragarðsgestur
 c) mauraæta
 d) mamaldýr

Word Quiz #191 - Zoo

Choose the best Icelandic word to match the English word.

1) bear
a) fjallaljón
b) tegundir
c) björn
d) sebrahestur

2) outdoor enclosure
a) utandyra girðing
b) kengúra
c) dýr
d) rándýr

3) fierce
a) kengúra
b) fíll
c) grimmilegur
d) úlfur

4) panda
a) panda
b) flóðhestur
c) jarðneskur
d) refur

5) aquatic
a) utandyra girðing
b) dagdýr
c) sædýr
d) flóðhestur

6) hippopotamus
a) kóalabjörn
b) skriðdýr
c) kengúra
d) flóðhestur

7) hyena
a) fjallaljón
b) hyena
c) gorilla
d) glerbúr

8) giraffe house
a) hryggleysingjar
b) jaguar
c) gíraffahús
d) grimmilegur

9) aardvark
a) dagdýr
b) jarðneskur
c) rándýr
d) mammaldýr

10) zebra
a) fílahús
b) aðgangur
c) dýragarðsvörður
d) sebrahestur

Word Quiz #192 - Zoo

Choose the best Icelandic word to match the English word.

1) vertebrate
   a) hryggleysingjar
   b) jaguar
   c) kóalabjörn
   d) mamaldýr

2) elephant enclosure
   a) glerbúr
   b) fílagirðing
   c) björn
   d) skriðdýr

3) mammal
   a) jarðneskur
   b) mamaldýr
   c) dýragarður
   d) hyena

4) baboon
   a) krókódíll
   b) dýragarðsgestur
   c) bavían
   d) fílagirðing

5) poisonous
   a) utandyra girðing
   b) eitraður
   c) kengúra
   d) girðing

6) outside cage
   a) sædýr
   b) úlfur
   c) jaguar
   d) utandyra búr

7) elephant
   a) refur
   b) fíll
   c) api
   d) kóalabjörn

8) animal
   a) sebrahestur
   b) rándýr
   c) dýr
   d) blettatígur

9) anteater
   a) mauraæta
   b) björn
   c) krókódíll
   d) mammaldýr

10) fierce
   a) ljón
   b) krókódíll
   c) apahús
   d) grimmilegur

Word Quiz #193 - Zoo

Choose the best Icelandic word to match the English word.

1) kangaroo
- a) hjörtur
- b) kengúra
- c) jurtaæta
- d) sædýr

2) hippopotamus
- a) aðgangur
- b) pardusdýr
- c) flóðhestur
- d) mauraæta

3) cougar
- a) apahús
- b) utandyra búr
- c) hættulegur
- d) fjallaljón

4) glass case
- a) dýragarður
- b) glerbúr
- c) girðing
- d) hryggleysingjar

5) reptile
- a) kóalabjörn
- b) skriðdýr
- c) aðgangur
- d) girðing

6) dangerous
- a) hættulegur
- b) girðing
- c) froskdýr
- d) grimmilegur

7) aviary
- a) björn
- b) dagdýr
- c) fuglasafn
- d) blettatígur

8) wolf
- a) krókódíll
- b) jurtaæta
- c) jarðneskur
- d) úlfur

9) panda
- a) dýragarður
- b) pardusdýr
- c) fjallaljón
- d) panda

10) jaguar
- a) jaguar
- b) dagdýr
- c) tegundir
- d) fílahús

Word Quiz #194 - Zoo

Choose the best Icelandic word to match the English word.

1) aquarium
  a) hyena
  b) sædýrabúr
  c) gíraffahús
  d) hættulegur

2) monkey house
  a) apahús
  b) beltisdýr
  c) mauraæta
  d) kóalabjörn

3) enclosing wall
  a) girðing
  b) panda
  c) gorilla
  d) blettatígur

4) gorilla
  a) gorilla
  b) apahús
  c) glerbúr
  d) girðing

5) reptile enclosure
  a) skriðdýragirðing
  b) glerbúr
  c) kóalabjörn
  d) fjallaljón

6) lion
  a) girðing
  b) froskdýr
  c) ljón
  d) mauraæta

7) vertebrate
  a) grimmilegur
  b) gíraffi
  c) dýr
  d) hryggleysingjar

8) giraffe
  a) utandyra búr
  b) gíraffi
  c) fílahús
  d) utandyra girðing

9) zebra
  a) fíll
  b) froskdýr
  c) sebrahestur
  d) fílahús

10) cougar
  a) fjallaljón
  b) eitraður
  c) sædýrabúr
  d) refur

Word Quiz #195 - Zoo

Choose the best Icelandic word to match the English word.

1) armadillo
   a) hjörtur
   b) jaguar
   c) beltisdýr
   d) rándýr

2) bear
   a) sædýrabúr
   b) dýragarðsvörður
   c) björn
   d) hættulegur

3) amphibian
   a) dýragarður
   b) skriðdýr
   c) apahús
   d) froskdýr

4) lion
   a) ljón
   b) hyena
   c) fuglasafn
   d) aðgangur

5) arboreal
   a) dýragarðsgestur
   b) blettatígur
   c) utandyra búr
   d) trjábýll

6) monkey
   a) ljón
   b) dagdýr
   c) fuglasafn
   d) api

7) zoo visitor
   a) girðing
   b) mauraæta
   c) dýragarðsgestur
   d) skriðdýragirðing

8) enclosing wall
   a) dagdýr
   b) krókódíll
   c) jaguar
   d) girðing

9) reptile enclosure
   a) glerbúr
   b) skriðdýragirðing
   c) fjallaljón
   d) grimmilegur

10) jaguar
   a) jarðneskur
   b) jaguar
   c) glerbúr
   d) panda

Word Quiz #196 - Zoo

Choose the best Icelandic word to match the English word.

1) fox
a) refur
b) fjallaljón
c) tegundir
d) kengúra

2) kangaroo
a) utandyra búr
b) kengúra
c) sebrahestur
d) rándýr

3) crocodile
a) dýragarðsgestur
b) krókódíll
c) aðgangur
d) kengúra

4) koala
a) krókódíll
b) úlfur
c) kóalabjörn
d) fíll

5) dangerous
a) flóðhestur
b) ljón
c) hættulegur
d) kengúra

6) giraffe
a) aðgangur
b) nashyrningur
c) gíraffi
d) kóalabjörn

7) outside cage
a) gíraffahús
b) utandyra búr
c) gorilla
d) björn

8) enclosing wall
a) dýr
b) blettatígur
c) sebrahestur
d) girðing

9) hippopotamus
a) flóðhestur
b) aðgangur
c) hættulegur
d) dýragarðsgestur

10) cheetah
a) kóalabjörn
b) sædýr
c) blettatígur
d) dýr

Word Quiz #197 - Zoo

Choose the best Icelandic word to match the English word.

1) zoo visitor
   a) tegundir
   b) dýragarðsgestur
   c) dagdýr
   d) dýragarður

2) elephant house
   a) apahús
   b) glerbúr
   c) fílahús
   d) sædýr

3) armadillo
   a) fuglasafn
   b) api
   c) beltisdýr
   d) flóðhestur

4) outdoor enclosure
   a) hlébarði
   b) rándýr
   c) trjábýll
   d) utandyra girðing

5) elephant
   a) fíll
   b) apahús
   c) sædýrabúr
   d) hjörtur

6) bear
   a) girðing
   b) panda
   c) björn
   d) jarðneskur

7) cougar
   a) jarðneskur
   b) fjallaljón
   c) mammaldýr
   d) gíraffi

8) mammal
   a) mamaldýr
   b) gíraffahús
   c) hyena
   d) utandyra búr

9) dangerous
   a) gíraffahús
   b) hættulegur
   c) dagdýr
   d) rándýr

10) zebra
   a) næturdýr
   b) sebrahestur
   c) fuglasafn
   d) kóalabjörn

Word Quiz #198 - Zoo

Choose the best Icelandic word to match the English word.

1) nocturnal
 a) pardusdýr
 b) næturdýr
 c) krókódíll
 d) glerbúr

2) aardvark
 a) hættulegur
 b) kóalabjörn
 c) jarðneskur
 d) mammaldýr

3) carnivore
 a) rándýr
 b) sædýrabúr
 c) trjábýll
 d) hlébarði

4) outdoor enclosure
 a) úlfur
 b) utandyra girðing
 c) gíraffi
 d) glerbúr

5) gazelle
 a) hjörtur
 b) glerbúr
 c) skriðdýr
 d) tígur

6) zookeeper
 a) dýragarðsvörður
 b) dýragarður
 c) skriðdýr
 d) beltisdýr

7) aviary
 a) fuglasafn
 b) dýragarður
 c) mammaldýr
 d) gíraffahús

8) terrestrial
 a) fílahús
 b) jarðneskur
 c) apahús
 d) fjallaljón

9) cheetah
 a) glerbúr
 b) mauraæta
 c) aðgangur
 d) blettatígur

10) crocodile
 a) krókódíll
 b) gorilla
 c) eitraður
 d) beltisdýr

Word Quiz #199 - Zoo

Choose the best Icelandic word to match the English word.

1) reptile enclosure
 a) dýragarðsvörður
 b) skriðdýragirðing
 c) panda
 d) tegundir

2) herbivore
 a) bavían
 b) jurtaæta
 c) úlfur
 d) blettatígur

3) koala
 a) mamaldýr
 b) sædýrabúr
 c) björn
 d) kóalabjörn

4) zoo
 a) dýragarður
 b) kóalabjörn
 c) úlfur
 d) grimmilegur

5) alligator
 a) tígur
 b) sebrahestur
 c) krókódíll
 d) fuglasafn

6) gorilla
 a) fuglasafn
 b) hættulegur
 c) gorilla
 d) mammaldýr

7) species
 a) beltisdýr
 b) tegundir
 c) kóalabjörn
 d) flóðhestur

8) leopard
 a) dagdýr
 b) hlébarði
 c) gorilla
 d) aðgangur

9) vertebrate
 a) kengúra
 b) hryggleysingjar
 c) froskdýr
 d) úlfur

10) kangaroo
 a) tígur
 b) kengúra
 c) dýragarðsvörður
 d) skriðdýragirðing

Word Quiz #200 - Zoo

Choose the best Icelandic word to match the English word.

1) poisonous
 a) grimmilegur
 b) kóalabjörn
 c) eitraður
 d) jarðneskur

2) alligator
 a) utandyra girðing
 b) gorilla
 c) panda
 d) krókódíll

3) leopard
 a) mamaldýr
 b) hryggleysingjar
 c) hlébarði
 d) mauraæta

4) anteater
 a) mammaldýr
 b) trjábýll
 c) panda
 d) mauraæta

5) giraffe house
 a) jurtaæta
 b) gíraffahús
 c) dýragarður
 d) utandyra búr

6) lion
 a) krókódíll
 b) ljón
 c) api
 d) froskdýr

7) enclosing wall
 a) sædýrabúr
 b) kengúra
 c) fíll
 d) girðing

8) koala
 a) mauraæta
 b) kóalabjörn
 c) rándýr
 d) gíraffahús

9) reptile enclosure
 a) blettatígur
 b) skriðdýragirðing
 c) gorilla
 d) sædýr

10) rhinoceros
 a) kóalabjörn
 b) nashyrningur
 c) dýr
 d) skriðdýr

Welcome to the solutions section!

Here you can find the answers to the quizzes.

Word Quiz Solutions

#1 - 1) d - to book   2) c - round trip ticket   3) d - security
4) c - altitude   5) a - tray   6) b - hangar   7) d - ticket   8) b - single
ticket   9) a - domestic   10) a - luggage

#2 - 1) d - destination   2) a - runway   3) d - tray   4) b - emergency
5) d - arrival   6) d - airport   7) b - rucksack   8) a - seat   9) a - weight
10) a - round trip ticket

#3 - 1) b - toilet   2) b - information   3) a - headphones   4) b - gate
5) b - departure   6) b - window   7) c - emergency   8) b - to declare
9) c - check-in   10) c - round trip ticket

#4 - 1) a - wing   2) c - window   3) d - helipad   4) d - gate
5) a - passport   6) a - economy class   7) b - air hostess
8) a - security   9) b - exit   10) a - to take off

#5 - 1) a - economy class   2) a - stewardess   3) a - runway
4) d - nonstop   5) b - to land   6) c - flight   7) a - metal detector
8) c - connection   9) c - early   10) c - air hostess

#6 - 1) c - single ticket   2) c - altitude   3) d - hangar
4) b - information   5) c - economy class   6) c - departure
7) b - wing   8) b - international   9) d - luggage   10) c - to land

#7 - 1) d - runway   2) c - helipad   3) b - international   4) a - life
preserver   5) a - first class   6) c - to cancel   7) b - departure
8) b - duty-free   9) b - to declare   10) a - to book

#8 - 1) b - airport   2) d - travel agency   3) a - to check bags
4) c - crew   5) d - flying   6) c - life preserver   7) c - helicopter
8) c - check-in   9) b - exit   10) d - duty-free

Word Quiz Solutions

#9 - 1) a - hangar   2) b - boarding pass   3) a - copilot
 4) c - international   5) d - helicopter   6) d - domestic
 7) a - passenger   8) a - land   9) c - ticket agent   10) d - to book

#10 - 1) a - toilet   2) c - international   3) c - gangway   4) c - nonstop
 5) d - passenger   6) c - gate   7) b - late   8) b - weight
 9) c - information   10) b - to fly

#11 - 1) b - seat   2) a - connection   3) a - weight   4) c - domestic
 5) d - copilot   6) a - flight   7) a - ticket   8) d - life preserver
 9) b - duty-free   10) d - ticket agent

#12 - 1) d - economy class   2) d - to land   3) b - to carry   4) c - duty-
free   5) a - luggage   6) b - rucksack   7) c - stewardess   8) c - to check
bags   9) b - window   10) a - round trip ticket

#13 - 1) b - duty-free   2) b - helicopter   3) c - ticket   4) d - round trip
ticket   5) a - toilet   6) a - weight   7) b - seat   8) c - take off   9) d - to
check bags   10) c - information

#14 - 1) d - miði báðar leiðir   2) c - koma   3) a - snemma
 4) d - öryggisvörður   5) a - að vera með sér   6) b - flugvöllur
 7) b - að taka á loft   8) b - að lýsa yfir   9) b - flugskýli
 10) a - farangur

#15 - 1) d - að lýsa yfir   2) c - almennt farrými   3) d - þyrlupallur
 4) a - aðstoðarflugmaður   5) b - öryggisvörður   6) d - snemma
 7) c - alþjóðlegt   8) b - björgunarvesti   9) b - beint flug
 10) b - flugbraut

#16 - 1) d - fyrsta flokks farrými   2) a - flugmaður   3) b - sæti
 4) b - snemma   5) d - farþegi   6) d - bakpoki   7) d - klósett
 8) b - innanlands   9) b - fljúga   10) c - súrefni

Word Quiz Solutions

#17 - 1) b - áfangastaður   2) b - göngubrú   3) b - miðasala
  4) d - hæð   5) d - tenging   6) a - að setjast niður   7) a - klósett
  8) a - flug   9) d - útgangur   10) b - ferðaþjónusta

#18 - 1) d - áfangastaður   2) d - flugmaður   3) c - að fljúga
  4) b - heyrnartól   5) a - flugtak   6) b - þyngd   7) d - skjalataska
  8) d - að setjast niður   9) d - fljúga   10) c - flugskýli

#19 - 1) d - að stimpla inn töskur   2) a - heyrnartól   3) a - beint
  4) d - flugvél   5) a - aðstoðarflugmaður   6) c - sæti
  7) d - löggæslumaður   8) b - bakpoki   9) d - skjalataska
  10) c - tollfrjáls

#20 - 1) c - miði aðra leið   2) d - kerra   3) d - koma
  4) d - upplýsingar   5) d - hjól   6) b - björgunarvesti   7) a - sæti
  8) a - flugbraut   9) d - tenging   10) c - flugvél

#21 - 1) c - þyrla   2) d - innanlands   3) d - að fljúga   4) c - brottför
  5) a - áfangastaður   6) a - miði aðra leið   7) d - miði báðar leiðir
  8) b - að setjast niður   9) b - vængur   10) a - björgunarvesti

#22 - 1) b - flugvöllur   2) d - þyrlupallur   3) d - að lýsa yfir
  4) b - björgunarvesti   5) a - að hætta við   6) d - útgangur   7) d - að
bóka   8) d - brottfararspjald   9) c - hæð   10) d - ferðaþjónusta

#23 - 1) d - almennt farrými   2) c - að lenda   3) b - flugtak
  4) d - fljúga   5) d - göngubrú   6) d - að taka á loft   7) a - beint
  8) c - bakpoki   9) d - áhöfn   10) b - miðasala

#24 - 1) b - hæð   2) c - að bóka   3) a - snemma   4) d - beint flug
  5) c - alþjóðlegt   6) d - land   7) b - seinn   8) b - útgangur
  9) b - þyrla   10) b - að taka á loft

Word Quiz Solutions

#25 - 1) a - að stimpla inn töskur   2) a - útgangur   3) a - seinn
 4) a - miði   5) a - að hætta við   6) c - flugvél   7) b - flugfreyja
 8) c - vegabréf   9) c - að lýsa yfir   10) c - miði aðra leið

#26 - 1) c - savings account   2) a - savings   3) d - travellers cheque
 4) a - bank account   5) d - payment   6) c - profit   7) d - to deposit
 8) a - current account   9) b - share   10) d - alarm

#27 - 1) c - safe deposit box   2) d - share   3) b - exchange rate
 4) d - contract   5) c - profit   6) d - to sign   7) c - money   8) c - guard
 9) d - bank account   10) b - customer

#28 - 1) c - account   2) d - percentage   3) b - money   4) c - account
balance   5) b - interest   6) b - credit card   7) d - euros   8) a - funds
transfer   9) b - dollars   10) b - to change

#29 - 1) d - amount   2) c - deposit   3) b - exchange rate   4) b - ATM
 5) a - savings account   6) a - withdrawal   7) c - profit
 8) b - customer   9) c - bank statement   10) b - to lend

#30 - 1) a - to pay   2) b - cheque   3) d - exchange rate   4) c - account
balance   5) d - credit   6) b - profit   7) a - cash   8) b - invoice
 9) b - transactions   10) a - to borrow

#31 - 1) d - coin   2) b - manager   3) a - to sign   4) a - exchange rate
 5) b - withdrawal   6) c - loan   7) a - debit card   8) d - to transfer
 9) c - bank   10) b - to lend

#32 - 1) b - bank   2) c - chequebook   3) d - interest   4) b - share
 5) b - currency   6) b - loan   7) a - deposit   8) b - fee   9) b - money
10) d - vault

Word Quiz Solutions

#33 - 1) b - balance   2) d - customer   3) b - account balance
 4) d - savings account   5) b - debt   6) a - amount   7) c - to borrow
 8) b - bank   9) d - manager   10) a - withdrawal

#34 - 1) a - to borrow   2) b - interest   3) b - percentage
 4) d - money   5) d - savings account   6) d - purchase   7) c - cash
 8) c - dollars   9) b - euros   10) d - travellers cheque

#35 - 1) c - change   2) c - to sign   3) a - expenses   4) d - credit
 5) d - payment   6) b - to deposit   7) c - vault   8) a - guard
 9) c - loan   10) c - manager

#36 - 1) a - safe   2) c - cashier   3) c - loss   4) a - to withdraw
 5) c - exchange rate   6) c - credit card   7) b - to transfer
 8) b - percentage   9) b - to pay   10) d - savings

#37 - 1) c - bank   2) c - profit   3) c - cashier   4) d - funds transfer
 5) d - capital   6) a - euros   7) c - manager   8) d - to withdraw
 9) a - value   10) b - savings

#38 - 1) d - cashier   2) b - cheque   3) c - guard   4) a - to lend
 5) c - invoice   6) b - withdrawal   7) c - bank   8) b - loss   9) c - debit
card   10) b - current account

#39 - 1) a - fjármagn   2) d - sparnaður   3) b - bankastaða
 4) d - gjaldmiðill   5) a - millifærsla   6) d - innheimta   7) c - að draga
inn   8) b - sparnaðarreikningur   9) c - staða   10) a - öryggisskápur

#40 - 1) a - útgjöld   2) a - gjaldmiðlavirði   3) c - skuld
 4) a - núverandi aðgangur   5) b - geymsla   6) b - gjaldmiðlaskipti
 7) b - samningur   8) c - færslur   9) d - öryggisskápur
 10) a - fjármagn

Word Quiz Solutions

#41 - 1) c - tap   2) a - gróði   3) c - að skrifa undir   4) a - vextir
5) b - öryggisskápur   6) a - sparnaðarreikningur   7) d - hlutabréf
8) a - hraðbanki   9) c - að draga inn   10) d - bankastaða

#42 - 1) b - staða   2) b - afgangur   3) b - öryggisvörður   4) d - að
millifæra   5) b - aðgangur   6) d - innlögn   7) d - sparnaðarreikningur
8) d - fjármagn   9) d - peningur   10) c - virði

#43 - 1) d - að fá lánað   2) d - bankayfirlit   3) b - tap   4) c - lánstraust
5) c - að Skipta   6) b - bankastaða   7) a - dollarar   8) a - gróði
9) d - kreditkort   10) b - að skrifa undir

#44 - 1) d - fjármagn   2) c - sparnaður   3) a - fjárhæð
4) d - ferðatékki   5) a - dollarar   6) c - gjaldmiðill   7) a - úttekt
8) b - geymsla   9) a - afgreiðslumaður   10) a - banki

#45 - 1) a - gjaldmiðlaskipti   2) b - geymsla   3) d - gjaldmiðill
4) b - öryggiskerfi   5) c - seðill   6) c - staða   7) c - að lána   8) a - tap
9) b - millifærsla   10) d - peningur

#46 - 1) b - afgangur   2) b - banki   3) d - gjaldkeri   4) c - prósenta
5) a - öryggiskerfi   6) c - að borga   7) c - hraðbanki   8) a - millifærsla
9) c - fjármagn   10) c - úttekt

#47 - 1) d - veðsetning   2) b - að draga inn   3) c - aðgangur
4) c - millifærsla   5) d - bankastaða   6) c - bankayfirlit   7) a - að
leggja inn   8) a - tap   9) b - gjald   10) b - innlögn

#48 - 1) c - að Skipta   2) b - núverandi aðgangur   3) a - að leggja inn
4) c - úttekt   5) b - afrit   6) d - kreditkort   7) a - aðgangur
8) c - debetkort   9) d - hlutabréf   10) b - gjaldkeri

Word Quiz Solutions

#49 - 1) a - öryggisskápur   2) b - gjaldmiðill   3) b - prósenta
 4) d - kreditkort   5) d - banki   6) c - gjaldmiðlavirði   7) c - vextir
 8) d - bankayfirlit   9) d - tap   10) a - seðill

#50 - 1) d - gjaldmiðlaskipti   2) b - fjármagn   3) c - kaup
 4) a - greiðsla   5) d - viðskiptavinur   6) d - tap   7) a - lán   8) c - seðill
 9) a - klink   10) b - gjald

#51 - 1) b - suite   2) d - hotel   3) d - view   4) b - room service
 5) c - living room   6) c - staircase   7) d - swimming pool
 8) c - message   9) c - recreation   10) c - booking

#52 - 1) b - carpet   2) c - reception desk   3) a - internet   4) b - ground
floor   5) d - complaint   6) b - room   7) c - lift   8) c - staircase
 9) c - bed   10) c - price

#53 - 1) d - suite   2) a - booking   3) a - staircase   4) d - hotel
 5) b - lobby   6) b - bill   7) b - ice   8) c - internet   9) c - doorman
 10) d - air conditioning

#54 - 1) a - chair   2) a - breakfast   3) c - bill   4) b - ice
 5) d - complaint   6) d - message   7) b - pillow   8) d - room service
 9) a - blanket   10) d - lobby

#55 - 1) d - lobby   2) b - price   3) d - view   4) a - stairs   5) b - carpet
 6) c - dining room   7) d - complaint   8) d - doorman   9) d - loo
 10) d - garage

#56 - 1) d - hotel   2) c - lift   3) c - stairs   4) d - suite   5) d - garage
 6) d - blanket   7) a - dining room   8) c - bed   9) a - lobby
 10) d - entrance

Word Quiz Solutions

#57 - 1) b - lift   2) a - recreation   3) b - internet   4) c - reception desk
 5) b - view   6) c - garage   7) d - swimming pool   8) b - hotel
 9) b - floor   10) d - checkout

#58 - 1) d - bed   2) a - stairs   3) d - reception desk   4) d - taxi
 5) b - receptionist   6) d - ground floor   7) a - recreation   8) a - bill
 9) d - lobby   10) a - bellboy

#59 - 1) a - view   2) a - chair   3) c - ice   4) c - bed   5) a - pillow
 6) c - price   7) a - loo   8) d - garage   9) b - blanket   10) b - stairs

#60 - 1) b - room service   2) b - bed   3) a - key   4) a - table
 5) c - message   6) d - internet   7) b - receptionist   8) b - staircase
 9) d - doorman   10) b - chair

#61 - 1) a - carpet   2) a - pillow   3) c - message   4) d - stairs
 5) b - suite   6) c - view   7) a - breakfast   8) c - room service
 9) a - staircase   10) a - hotel

#62 - 1) d - taxi   2) a - breakfast   3) b - entrance   4) c - price
 5) a - complaint   6) b - loo   7) b - bed   8) a - key   9) b - hotel
 10) c - doorman

#63 - 1) b - recreation   2) a - doorman   3) c - checkout   4) b - suite
 5) a - garage   6) c - staircase   7) a - air conditioning   8) d - key
 9) d - booking   10) d - pillow

#64 - 1) a - verð   2) d - jarðhæð   3) a - endurgerð   4) d - stofa
 5) b - stigar   6) b - útsýni   7) d - kvörtun   8) c - gestamóttaka
 9) d - reikningur   10) c - vikapiltur

Word Quiz Solutions

#65 - 1) a - stóll   2) b - verð   3) c - rúm   4) b - stigar   5) b - jarðhæð
6) c - móttaka   7) a - herbergisþjónusta   8) a - hæð   9) c - matsalur
10) a - hotel

#66 - 1) a - verð   2) a - endurgerð   3) b - þerna   4) d - hæð
5) c - inngangur   6) d - dyravörður   7) d - lyfta   8) d - vikapiltur
9) d - teppi   10) b - útsýni

#67 - 1) d - herbergi   2) a - gestamóttaka   3) d - sundlaug
4) c - svalir   5) a - leigubíll   6) c - loftræsting   7) b - afgreiðsla
8) a - útsýni   9) d - ís   10) b - reikningur

#68 - 1) d - lyfta   2) c - stofa   3) d - móttaka   4) b - ís   5) a - lykill
6) d - internet   7) d - þerna   8) c - verð   9) c - svíta   10) b - vikapiltur

#69 - 1) c - dyravörður   2) c - vikapiltur   3) a - borð   4) b - lykill
5) a - verð   6) a - bílskúr   7) d - skilaboð   8) c - sundlaug
9) d - gestamóttaka   10) c - stigar

#70 - 1) a - bílskúr   2) a - svíta   3) b - hotel   4) d - móttaka
5) c - loftræsting   6) a - matsalur   7) c - gestamóttakandi
8) a - endurgerð   9) b - internet   10) d - koddi

#71 - 1) b - verð   2) d - þerna   3) a - stigar   4) b - stofa   5) a - stigar
6) a - bókun   7) c - teppi   8) d - dyravörður   9) a - herbergi
10) d - skilaboð

#72 - 1) b - rúm   2) d - borð   3) c - teppi   4) c - internet   5) d - stofa
6) b - hæð   7) a - gestamóttaka   8) b - útsýni   9) d - verð
10) a - bílskúr

Word Quiz Solutions

#73 - 1) c - reikningur   2) c - sundlaug   3) a - stóll   4) a - verð
 5) a - herbergi   6) a - jarðhæð   7) d - svíta   8) c - móttaka
 9) b - stigar   10) b - leigubíll

#74 - 1) d - stigar   2) c - borð   3) c - morgunmatur   4) b - leigubíll
 5) a - útsýni   6) a - teppi   7) c - gestamóttakandi   8) c - loftræsting
 9) a - reikningur   10) d - stóll

#75 - 1) d - sundlaug   2) c - gestamóttaka   3) c - bókun   4) b - bílskúr
 5) d - loftræsting   6) c - þerna   7) a - rúm   8) c - vikapiltur
 9) c - borð   10) d - afgreiðsla

#76 - 1) a - bandage   2) c - injection   3) d - pill   4) b - syrup
 5) c - antibiotic   6) b - pharmacy   7) b - thermometer   8) d - vitamin
 9) a - prescription   10) c - ointment

#77 - 1) a - vitamin   2) d - antibiotic   3) c - pill   4) d - bandage
 5) d - injection   6) b - medicine   7) b - pharmacist   8) a - cortisone
 9) c - laxative   10) a - thermometer

#78 - 1) d - iodine   2) b - antibiotic   3) d - thermometer
 4) c - vitamin   5) d - pharmacy   6) d - injection   7) c - prescription
 8) d - dental floss   9) c - insulin   10) d - bandage

#79 - 1) d - iodine   2) d - pharmacist   3) d - laxative
 4) c - prescription   5) c - cortisone   6) b - penicillin   7) a - dental
floss   8) a - vitamin   9) a - insulin   10) d - medicine

#80 - 1) d - aspirin   2) d - laxative   3) b - syrup   4) a - tablet
 5) c - insulin   6) d - vitamin   7) b - prescription   8) c - penicillin
 9) b - injection   10) c - pharmacy

Word Quiz Solutions

#81 - 1) c - medicine   2) d - bandage   3) c - injection   4) d - laxative
5) a - pharmacist   6) b - prescription   7) a - aspirin   8) a - vitamin
9) a - penicillin   10) a - ointment

#82 - 1) c - iodine   2) a - laxative   3) c - thermometer
4) b - medicine   5) d - pill   6) b - syrup   7) d - prescription
8) b - insulin   9) a - antibiotic   10) c - pharmacist

#83 - 1) a - pharmacy   2) d - tablet   3) c - medicine   4) d - vitamin
5) b - aspirin   6) c - syrup   7) b - thermometer   8) b - cortisone
9) a - iodine   10) b - laxative

#84 - 1) b - penicillin   2) a - pharmacist   3) a - bandage   4) c - tablet
5) c - syrup   6) a - aspirin   7) d - pharmacy   8) b - ointment
9) a - medicine   10) b - injection

#85 - 1) d - bandage   2) c - vitamin   3) c - iodine   4) d - pill
5) d - prescription   6) d - pharmacy   7) d - ointment
8) d - thermometer   9) d - insulin   10) c - syrup

#86 - 1) c - pill   2) d - cortisone   3) d - ointment   4) c - tablet
5) c - laxative   6) d - aspirin   7) b - injection   8) a - iodine
9) c - dental floss   10) d - vitamin

#87 - 1) b - dental floss   2) b - antibiotic   3) a - pill
4) b - prescription   5) b - iodine   6) b - penicillin   7) a - cortisone
8) c - vitamin   9) a - pharmacist   10) d - syrup

#88 - 1) d - ointment   2) d - penicillin   3) b - insulin   4) d - iodine
5) c - pill   6) b - prescription   7) a - vitamin   8) c - bandage
9) b - pharmacy   10) b - injection

Word Quiz Solutions

#89 - 1) a - munnskol   2) c - sýklalyf   3) c - hægðalyf   4) b - kortisón
5) d - sýróp   6) d - læknir   7) b - insulin   8) c - tafla   9) b - tafla
10) c - aspirin

#90 - 1) d - kortisón   2) b - apótek   3) a - hægðalyf   4) d - tafla
5) c - munnskol   6) c - sýklalyf   7) b - tafla   8) b - plástur
9) c - áburður   10) d - lyfseðill

#91 - 1) d - áburður   2) d - kortisón   3) a - joð   4) c - vítamín
5) c - insulin   6) d - hægðalyf   7) a - sýklalyf   8) c - plástur
9) a - lyfseðill   10) b - hitamælir

#92 - 1) c - lyfseðill   2) a - læknir   3) a - pensilín   4) b - kortisón
5) c - insulin   6) c - plástur   7) c - hitamælir   8) a - innspýting
9) a - apótek   10) d - áburður

#93 - 1) d - apótek   2) a - hitamælir   3) a - læknir   4) d - innspýting
5) c - lyf   6) b - munnskol   7) a - kortisón   8) a - plástur   9) c - tafla
10) a - hægðalyf

#94 - 1) b - munnskol   2) d - innspýting   3) d - vítamín   4) c - áburður
5) c - lyfseðill   6) d - pensilín   7) c - insulin   8) d - sýróp   9) b - lyf
10) c - aspirin

#95 - 1) b - sýklalyf   2) b - hægðalyf   3) a - hitamælir   4) c - pensilín
5) b - tafla   6) b - munnskol   7) c - apótek   8) a - innspýting
9) d - kortisón   10) d - insulin

#96 - 1) c - tafla   2) c - vítamín   3) a - áburður   4) b - kortisón
5) b - plástur   6) b - insulin   7) d - hægðalyf   8) b - hitamælir
9) c - aspirin   10) a - lyf

Word Quiz Solutions

#97 - 1) b - insulin   2) b - sýróp   3) b - kortisón   4) a - aspirin
  5) c - munnskol   6) c - læknir   7) a - joð   8) a - plástur   9) b - lyfseðill
  10) a - tafla

#98 - 1) b - vítamín   2) c - joð   3) a - lyfseðill   4) a - aspirin
  5) a - læknir   6) a - munnskol   7) a - plástur   8) c - tafla   9) d - sýróp
  10) a - apótek

#99 - 1) c - tafla   2) a - hitamælir   3) a - hægðalyf   4) b - pensilín
  5) c - tafla   6) a - kortisón   7) b - munnskol   8) d - apótek
  9) c - sýróp   10) b - joð

#100 - 1) d - plástur   2) d - insulin   3) c - lyfseðill   4) a - sýklalyf
  5) c - áburður   6) d - lyf   7) a - vítamín   8) d - læknir   9) d - pensilín
  10) a - aspirin

#101 - 1) b - Russia   2) d - Israel   3) c - Yugoslavia   4) d - Morocco
  5) a - Italy   6) b - Sweden   7) a - Netherlands   8) a - Switzerland
  9) c - China   10) c - Finland

#102 - 1) a - Ireland   2) c - Israel   3) b - China   4) a - Asia
  5) c - Canada   6) b - Luxembourg   7) c - Greece   8) b - France
  9) a - South Africa   10) b - New Zealand

#103 - 1) d - Israel   2) d - Ireland   3) b - Asia   4) d - Africa
  5) d - South Africa   6) d - North America   7) b - New Zealand
  8) a - Europe   9) a - Turkey   10) b - Sweden

#104 - 1) d - Asia   2) d - Turkey   3) c - Netherlands   4) b - South
Africa   5) a - Russia   6) a - Africa   7) a - Canada   8) d - Algeria
  9) c - South America   10) c - Israel

Word Quiz Solutions

#105 - 1) a - Yugoslavia 2) d - England 3) a - Austria 4) c - China 5) a - Slovenia 6) c - South America 7) d - Portugal 8) d - United States 9) c - Spain 10) b - Denmark

#106 - 1) a - Spain 2) b - Norway 3) a - Slovenia 4) d - Australia 5) c - Israel 6) c - Denmark 7) b - Ireland 8) d - Europe 9) a - England 10) a - Netherlands

#107 - 1) a - Scotland 2) a - Wales 3) c - Israel 4) a - Netherlands 5) b - Yugoslavia 6) c - Ireland 7) c - China 8) a - Turkey 9) b - Portugal 10) a - Africa

#108 - 1) a - South Africa 2) c - South America 3) c - Austria 4) c - Canada 5) b - England 6) c - Australia 7) b - Italy 8) b - France 9) d - Germany 10) d - Switzerland

#109 - 1) d - Israel 2) c - Turkey 3) a - Portugal 4) a - Netherlands 5) a - Ireland 6) b - Norway 7) d - Great Britain 8) d - Russia 9) d - Scotland 10) c - England

#110 - 1) a - Africa 2) b - Europe 3) a - England 4) b - South Africa 5) a - United States 6) d - Israel 7) d - Great Britain 8) c - Sweden 9) a - France 10) b - Austria

#111 - 1) b - Israel 2) b - Finland 3) b - Tunisia 4) c - Russia 5) c - Portugal 6) b - Sweden 7) a - Algeria 8) d - Yugoslavia 9) d - South America 10) c - France

#112 - 1) c - China 2) a - India 3) d - Asia 4) b - Germany 5) c - Algeria 6) a - England 7) c - Norway 8) a - Great Britain 9) a - Finland 10) a - Ireland

Word Quiz Solutions

#113 - 1) b - South America   2) a - England   3) d - Sweden
 4) a - Wales   5) b - Switzerland   6) c - Russia   7) d - Yugoslavia
 8) c - United States   9) b - Germany   10) a - Portugal

#114 - 1) c - Júgóslavía   2) c - Grikkland   3) a - Nýja Sjáland
 4) a - Afríka   5) a - Kína   6) d - Spánn   7) a - Indland   8) c - Austurríki
 9) d - Kanada   10) d - Noregur

#115 - 1) c - Austurríki   2) d - Rússland   3) c - Portúgal   4) b - Nýja
Sjáland   5) c - Indland   6) a - Ástralía   7) b - Algería   8) a - Kína
 9) d - Suður Ameríka   10) d - Írland

#116 - 1) a - Wales   2) a - Rússland   3) d - Kína   4) d - Ítalía
 5) d - Norður Ameríka   6) d - Nýja Sjáland   7) c - Austurríki
 8) d - Sviss   9) a - Svíþjóð   10) b - Afríka

#117 - 1) c - Suður Ameríka   2) d - Nýja Sjáland   3) a - Írland
 4) b - Sviss   5) c - Belgía   6) d - Suður Afríka   7) d - Morokkó
 8) d - Túnis   9) a - Þýskaland   10) c - Afríka

#118 - 1) c - Ítalía   2) c - Júgóslavía   3) c - Skotland   4) d - Bretland
 5) b - Morokkó   6) c - Þýskaland   7) b - Finnland   8) a - Tyrkland
 9) d - Lúxemborg   10) b - Portúgal

#119 - 1) b - Svíþjóð   2) c - Suður Ameríka   3) c - Ítalía   4) c - Algería
 5) c - Indland   6) d - Portúgal   7) c - Bretland   8) b - Wales
 9) c - Kanada   10) a - Norður Ameríka

#120 - 1) d - Noregur   2) a - Algería   3) d - Wales   4) c - Ítalía
 5) d - Lúxemborg   6) a - Kanada   7) c - Sviss   8) a - Ástralía
 9) a - Þýskaland   10) d - Afríka

Word Quiz Solutions

#121 - 1) d - Norður Ameríka   2) a - Rússland   3) c - Kína
 4) c - Algería   5) d - Tyrkland   6) a - Túnis   7) a - Írland
 8) c - Júgóslavía   9) a - Finnland   10) d - Wales

#122 - 1) d - Norður Ameríka   2) d - Svíþjóð   3) d - Evrópa
 4) d - Belgía   5) b - Túnis   6) a - Lúxemborg   7) d - Þýskaland
 8) d - Sviss   9) b - Suður Ameríka   10) c - Tyrkland

#123 - 1) d - Suður Afríka   2) d - Belgía   3) a - England
 4) d - Skotland   5) a - Holland   6) b - Afríka   7) d - Júgóslavía
 8) b - Túnis   9) d - Asía   10) c - Norður Ameríka

#124 - 1) b - Suður Ameríka   2) d - Tyrkland   3) a - Indland
 4) a - Frakkland   5) d - Bandaríkin   6) a - Danmörk   7) c - Asía
 8) d - Afríka   9) a - Skotland   10) b - Rússland

#125 - 1) b - Evrópa   2) d - Slóvenía   3) a - Holland   4) b - Asía
 5) b - Grikkland   6) d - Þýskaland   7) b - Japan   8) a - Suður Afríka
 9) c - Finnland   10) c - Bretland

#126 - 1) a - letter   2) d - envelope   3) a - to write   4) b - post
 5) d - money order   6) d - courier   7) b - clerk   8) b - to wait
 9) a - sender   10) b - to send

#127 - 1) d - registered letter   2) b - clerk   3) d - letter   4) d - to post
 5) c - package   6) d - import   7) c - courier   8) b - sender
 9) c - postman   10) d - airmail

#128 - 1) d - address   2) c - post   3) a - money order   4) d - to send
 5) a - reply   6) a - to wait   7) a - import   8) a - letterbox
 9) c - airmail   10) d - clerk

Word Quiz Solutions

#129 - 1) b - clerk   2) a - registered letter   3) d - courier   4) b - money order   5) c - import   6) b - to send   7) c - post   8) c - to post   9) a - to write   10) c - printed item

#130 - 1) a - address   2) c - import   3) d - post office   4) d - sender   5) c - to send   6) c - printed item   7) a - clerk   8) c - to write   9) a - airmail   10) c - note

#131 - 1) a - clerk   2) b - letter   3) d - package   4) c - note   5) d - reply   6) c - letterbox   7) c - money order   8) c - to post   9) c - address   10) d - registered letter

#132 - 1) a - envelope   2) b - sender   3) b - post office   4) c - to send   5) b - to write   6) b - letterbox   7) b - reply   8) b - registered letter   9) a - airmail   10) c - package

#133 - 1) b - post office   2) d - note   3) c - post   4) d - postage stamp   5) b - letterbox   6) b - to send   7) b - registered letter   8) c - money order   9) c - to post   10) a - postman

#134 - 1) a - letter   2) a - package   3) a - to write   4) b - courier   5) d - import   6) a - to send   7) b - letterbox   8) b - registered letter   9) b - export   10) a - post

#135 - 1) b - to post   2) d - registered letter   3) a - airmail   4) c - postman   5) c - address   6) d - package   7) a - reply   8) a - post office   9) a - clerk   10) b - to write

#136 - 1) b - import   2) a - letterbox   3) d - postage stamp   4) c - address   5) a - printed item   6) d - export   7) c - registered letter   8) d - to post   9) c - to wait   10) c - sender

Word Quiz Solutions

#137 - 1) b - airmail   2) b - postman   3) a - note   4) c - courier
5) d - to send   6) d - money order   7) c - post   8) b - post office
9) c - import   10) c - package

#138 - 1) d - reply   2) b - export   3) a - postman   4) a - letter
5) c - sender   6) a - envelope   7) a - to post   8) a - import
9) c - airmail   10) c - registered letter

#139 - 1) d - innflutningur   2) d - bréf   3) c - prentað bréf   4) c - að
senda   5) c - afgreiðslumaður   6) b - póstbox   7) b - útfluttningur
8) c - skráð bréf   9) a - að bíða   10) c - pósthús

#140 - 1) b - að deila   2) d - bréfberi   3) b - frímerki   4) b - sendandi
5) b - heimilisfang   6) b - skráð bréf   7) c - innflutningur   8) b - bréf
9) d - pósthús   10) b - póstur

#141 - 1) c - innflutningur   2) a - peningasending   3) a - flugpóstur
4) d - frímerki   5) d - prentað bréf   6) d - afgreiðslumaður
7) a - heimilisfang   8) b - pakki   9) c - bréf   10) a - að deila

#142 - 1) d - afgreiðslumaður   2) d - peningasending   3) b - að senda
4) d - svar   5) b - að deila   6) c - bréf   7) c - boðberi
8) c - heimilisfang   9) b - umslag   10) c - sendandi

#143 - 1) c - sendandi   2) c - bréf   3) b - að bíða   4) d - pakki
5) b - peningasending   6) c - afgreiðslumaður   7) a - útfluttningur
8) d - flugpóstur   9) a - póstur   10) d - svar

#144 - 1) c - pakki   2) b - frímerki   3) c - innflutningur
4) a - sendandi   5) d - prentað bréf   6) a - flugpóstur   7) d - að
senda   8) b - að skrifa   9) a - peningasending   10) c - póstur

Word Quiz Solutions

#145 - 1) c - svar   2) a - innflutningur   3) d - prentað bréf
 4) a - peningasending   5) a - útfluttningur   6) a - flugpóstur
 7) c - pakki   8) c - umslag   9) a - afgreiðslumaður   10) c - póstur

#146 - 1) a - skráð bréf   2) c - bréf   3) c - heimilisfang
 4) c - peningasending   5) b - að skrifa   6) d - að deila   7) d - prentað
bréf   8) d - pósthús   9) b - flugpóstur   10) d - sendandi

#147 - 1) b - að senda   2) c - svar   3) c - afgreiðslumaður   4) b - skráð
bréf   5) d - frímerki   6) b - innflutningur   7) c - heimilisfang
 8) b - póstur   9) a - bréfberi   10) b - flugpóstur

#148 - 1) c - innflutningur   2) a - bréfberi   3) d - flugpóstur
 4) d - bréf   5) a - frímerki   6) c - að deila   7) c - svar
 8) d - afgreiðslumaður   9) c - bréf   10) a - sendandi

#149 - 1) c - að bíða   2) b - frímerki   3) b - bréf   4) d - innflutningur
 5) a - bréfberi   6) b - að senda   7) b - peningasending   8) a - pakki
 9) a - afgreiðslumaður   10) a - skráð bréf

#150 - 1) d - heimilisfang   2) c - póstbox   3) c - innflutningur
 4) c - pósthús   5) d - útfluttningur   6) a - að senda   7) d - svar
 8) c - flugpóstur   9) d - póstur   10) d - bréf

#151 - 1) a - sea   2) d - jungle   3) c - marsh   4) a - environment
 5) b - bay   6) d - tide   7) d - beach   8) b - cave   9) c - gulf
 10) b - dam

#152 - 1) d - field   2) b - mountain   3) c - tide   4) d - forest
 5) b - coast   6) c - atmosphere   7) a - plain   8) b - meadow
 9) a - bay   10) d - island

Word Quiz Solutions

#153 - 1) c - sand   2) c - mountain   3) c - landscape   4) c - dam
5) c - canal   6) a - meadow   7) d - jungle   8) b - forest   9) d - cape
10) c - environment

#154 - 1) a - desert   2) c - tide   3) c - peninsula   4) d - dam
5) c - mountain   6) a - sea   7) a - canal   8) a - stone   9) a - coast
10) b - gulf

#155 - 1) a - dam   2) b - earthquake   3) b - bay   4) a - cape
5) b - atmosphere   6) d - sand   7) c - island   8) c - stone
9) a - desert   10) b - river

#156 - 1) d - nature   2) b - peninsula   3) b - sea   4) a - grass
5) b - gulf   6) a - dam   7) b - sand   8) b - plain   9) c - bay
10) a - stone

#157 - 1) d - stone   2) c - mountain   3) b - gulf   4) c - marsh
5) c - bay   6) d - coast   7) a - plain   8) b - jungle   9) a - sea
10) a - sand

#158 - 1) c - stone   2) c - peninsula   3) c - cape   4) c - earthquake
5) d - coast   6) d - grass   7) c - beach   8) a - nature   9) c - canal
10) c - field

#159 - 1) c - stone   2) c - forest   3) b - dam   4) c - jungle   5) b - bay
6) a - rock   7) c - marsh   8) a - peninsula   9) d - environment
10) b - earthquake

#160 - 1) a - rock   2) b - sand   3) a - field   4) b - forest   5) a - sea
6) c - coast   7) b - plain   8) c - marsh   9) b - meadow   10) b - desert

Word Quiz Solutions

#161 - 1) b - landscape   2) a - bay   3) b - desert   4) d - river
5) a - cave   6) d - coast   7) d - ocean   8) d - mountain   9) a - hill
10) d - lake

#162 - 1) d - sea   2) b - peninsula   3) d - dam   4) b - marsh
5) d - sand   6) a - jungle   7) c - forest   8) b - meadow
9) b - earthquake   10) d - gulf

#163 - 1) a - peninsula   2) c - ocean   3) a - plain   4) a - hill   5) c - tide
6) a - canal   7) c - dam   8) d - environment   9) a - pond
10) d - meadow

#164 - 1) b - gras   2) a - frumskógur   3) a - sjávarströnd
4) d - fjörður   5) a - hæð   6) a - gjá   7) b - hellir   8) b - skógur
9) b - haf   10) d - flatlendi

#165 - 1) c - skógur   2) a - haf   3) d - akur   4) a - gjá   5) b - lækur
6) a - flatlendi   7) c - steinn   8) a - engi   9) c - frumskógur
10) d - steinn

#166 - 1) c - fjörður   2) c - náttúra   3) b - skagi   4) c - steinn
5) c - strönd   6) b - tjörn   7) b - eyja   8) d - sjávarföll   9) d - sandur
10) b - mýri

#167 - 1) a - gras   2) a - stífla   3) b - fjörður   4) a - hæð   5) b - sjór
6) c - eyðimörk   7) c - engi   8) b - sveit   9) b - landslag   10) a - fjall

#168 - 1) d - frumskógur   2) b - steinn   3) b - skurður   4) a - stífla
5) b - hellir   6) d - steinn   7) c - sandur   8) b - sjávarströnd
9) b - gras   10) b - sveit

Word Quiz Solutions

#169 - 1) a - gjá   2) d - fjörður   3) a - flatlendi   4) a - andrúmsloft
5) b - sandur   6) a - steinn   7) c - sjávarföll   8) a - tjörn   9) c - eyja
10) d - sjór

#170 - 1) d - andrúmsloft   2) a - eyja   3) c - akur   4) a - fjall
5) d - mýri   6) b - engi   7) d - tjörn   8) b - stífla   9) b - landslag
10) c - gras

#171 - 1) b - hæð   2) a - sjávarföll   3) c - eyðimörk   4) b - umhverfi
5) c - lækur   6) c - andrúmsloft   7) a - landslag   8) b - skógur
9) b - haf   10) a - tjörn

#172 - 1) b - jarðskjálfti   2) c - sveit   3) c - mýri   4) c - fjörður
5) a - hellir   6) c - strönd   7) b - tjörn   8) c - sandur   9) a - gjá
10) a - flatlendi

#173 - 1) c - umhverfi   2) a - náttúra   3) d - sjór   4) c - andrúmsloft
5) d - eyja   6) d - fjörður   7) b - skurður   8) c - landslag   9) a - stífla
10) a - fjall

#174 - 1) a - skurður   2) c - andrúmsloft   3) d - eyja   4) b - mýri
5) b - sveit   6) d - á   7) c - sjór   8) c - lækur   9) d - landslag
10) b - sjávarströnd

#175 - 1) c - eyja   2) d - hellir   3) d - engi   4) b - á   5) c - hæð
6) c - sjávarströnd   7) a - akur   8) c - steinn   9) b - fjörður
10) b - steinn

#176 - 1) a - herbivore   2) c - leopard   3) c - fox   4) d - giraffe house
5) a - cougar   6) c - rhinoceros   7) a - baboon   8) d - animal
9) d - aardvark   10) a - amphibian

Word Quiz Solutions

#177 - 1) b - elephant enclosure   2) c - terrestrial   3) b - outdoor enclosure   4) c - lion   5) a - species   6) b - reptile   7) c - elephant   8) d - aviary   9) d - outside cage   10) c - crocodile

#178 - 1) d - hippopotamus   2) a - elephant   3) c - vertebrate   4) b - bear   5) a - gazelle   6) c - nocturnal   7) b - outside cage   8) c - gorilla   9) a - fox   10) c - admission

#179 - 1) c - reptile   2) a - zookeeper   3) c - elephant house   4) a - crocodile   5) c - panther   6) d - koala   7) d - zebra   8) b - cheetah   9) d - lion   10) b - kangaroo

#180 - 1) d - monkey   2) a - carnivore   3) b - reptile enclosure   4) a - giraffe   5) b - aquatic   6) a - panda   7) d - leopard   8) d - animal   9) a - hyena   10) a - outside cage

#181 - 1) d - reptile enclosure   2) a - aquarium   3) d - enclosing wall   4) c - giraffe   5) a - vertebrate   6) b - lion   7) d - fox   8) c - zebra   9) b - jaguar   10) d - crocodile

#182 - 1) a - giraffe   2) a - alligator   3) d - giraffe house   4) a - gazelle   5) c - aviary   6) c - panda   7) c - kangaroo   8) d - mammal   9) a - admission   10) a - monkey

#183 - 1) b - elephant enclosure   2) d - elephant   3) c - carnivore   4) a - dangerous   5) c - rhinoceros   6) a - kangaroo   7) a - wolf   8) c - enclosing wall   9) c - cougar   10) c - aardvark

#184 - 1) b - gorilla   2) b - animal   3) a - enclosing wall   4) c - armadillo   5) d - hyena   6) a - outside cage   7) a - nocturnal   8) b - bear   9) d - reptile   10) b - gazelle

Word Quiz Solutions

#185 - 1) b - gorilla 2) b - panda 3) d - leopard 4) b - armadillo
5) d - vertebrate 6) b - nocturnal 7) b - dangerous 8) c - monkey
9) d - fox 10) d - diurnal

#186 - 1) c - reptile 2) c - cougar 3) d - glass case 4) b - elephant
house 5) d - zookeeper 6) d - dangerous 7) b - lion 8) a - monkey
house 9) d - reptile enclosure 10) d - zoo

#187 - 1) b - anteater 2) b - amphibian 3) d - poisonous
4) c - zookeeper 5) d - bear 6) a - lion 7) d - armadillo
8) c - admission 9) a - arboreal 10) b - aardvark

#188 - 1) a - terrestrial 2) c - jaguar 3) a - tiger 4) c - baboon
5) b - hyena 6) b - species 7) d - glass case 8) d - giraffe house
9) c - gorilla 10) a - monkey house

#189 - 1) a - panda 2) c - fílagirðing 3) b - dýragarður
4) a - hættulegur 5) d - ljón 6) b - björn 7) d - dýragarðsvörður
8) c - beltisdýr 9) b - dýr 10) d - úlfur

#190 - 1) d - tígur 2) d - apahús 3) b - hjörtur 4) d - fílahús
5) b - fílagirðing 6) a - grimmilegur 7) c - björn 8) b - trjábýll
9) a - api 10) b - dýragarðsgestur

#191 - 1) c - björn 2) a - utandyra girðing 3) c - grimmilegur
4) a - panda 5) c - sædýr 6) d - flóðhestur 7) b - hyena
8) c - gíraffahús 9) d - mammaldýr 10) d - sebrahestur

#192 - 1) a - hryggleysingjar 2) b - fílagirðing 3) b - mamaldýr
4) c - bavían 5) b - eitraður 6) d - utandyra búr 7) b - fíll 8) c - dýr
9) a - mauraæta 10) d - grimmilegur

Word Quiz Solutions

#193 - 1) b - kengúra   2) c - flóðhestur   3) d - fjallaljón   4) b - glerbúr
5) b - skriðdýr   6) a - hættulegur   7) c - fuglasafn   8) d - úlfur
9) d - panda   10) a - jaguar

#194 - 1) b - sædýrabúr   2) a - apahús   3) a - girðing   4) a - gorilla
5) a - skriðdýragirðing   6) c - ljón   7) d - hryggleysingjar   8) b - gíraffi
9) c - sebrahestur   10) a - fjallaljón

#195 - 1) c - beltisdýr   2) c - björn   3) d - froskdýr   4) a - ljón
5) d - trjábýll   6) d - api   7) c - dýragarðsgestur   8) d - girðing
9) b - skriðdýragirðing   10) b - jaguar

#196 - 1) a - refur   2) b - kengúra   3) b - krókódíll   4) c - kóalabjörn
5) c - hættulegur   6) c - gíraffi   7) b - utandyra búr   8) d - girðing
9) a - flóðhestur   10) c - blettatígur

#197 - 1) b - dýragarðsgestur   2) c - fílahús   3) c - beltisdýr
4) d - utandyra girðing   5) a - fíll   6) c - björn   7) b - fjallaljón
8) a - mamaldýr   9) b - hættulegur   10) b - sebrahestur

#198 - 1) b - næturdýr   2) d - mammaldýr   3) a - rándýr
4) b - utandyra girðing   5) a - hjörtur   6) a - dýragarðsvörður
7) a - fuglasafn   8) b - jarðneskur   9) d - blettatígur   10) a - krókódíll

#199 - 1) b - skriðdýragirðing   2) b - jurtaæta   3) d - kóalabjörn
4) a - dýragarður   5) c - krókódíll   6) c - gorilla   7) b - tegundir
8) b - hlébarði   9) b - hryggleysingjar   10) b - kengúra

#200 - 1) c - eitraður   2) d - krókódíll   3) c - hlébarði
4) d - mauraæta   5) b - gíraffahús   6) b - ljón   7) d - girðing
8) b - kóalabjörn   9) b - skriðdýragirðing   10) b - nashyrningur

Welcome to the Dictionary section!

Icelandic words are given in bold, with the English meaning after.

Parts of speech are given in [].

m = masculine noun   mp = masculine plural

f = feminine noun   fp = feminine plural

n = neuter noun   np = neuter plural

adj = adjective   adv = adverb

num = number   v = verb

á *[f]* - river
áburður *[m]* - ointment
áfangastaður *[m]* - destination
afgangur *[m]* - change
afgreiðsla *[f]* - checkout
afgreiðslumaður *[m]* - cashier, clerk
Afríka - Africa
afrit *[n]* - receipt
áhöfn *[f]* - crew
akur *[m]* - field
Algería - Algeria
almennt farrými *[n]* - economy class
alþjóðlegt *[adj]* - international
andrúmsloft *[n]* - atmosphere
apahús *[n]* - monkey house
api *[m]* - monkey
apótek *[n]* - pharmacy
Asía - Asia
aspirin *[n]* - aspirin
Ástralía - Australia
Austurríki - Austria
að bíða *[v]* - to wait
að bóka *[v]* - to book
að borga *[v]* - to pay
að deila *[v]* - to post
að draga inn *[v]* - to cash
að fá lánað *[v]* - to borrow
að fara um borð *[v]* - to board
að fljúga *[v]* - to fly
að hætta við *[v]* - to cancel
að lána *[v]* - to lend
að leggja inn *[v]* - to deposit
að lenda *[v]* - to land
að lýsa yfir *[v]* - to declare
að millifæra *[v]* - to transfer
að senda *[v]* - to send

að setjast niður *[v]* - to sit down
að Skipta *[v]* - to change
að skrifa *[v]* - to write
að skrifa undir *[v]* - to sign
að stimpla inn töskur *[v]* - to check bags
að taka á loft *[v]* - to take off
að taka út *[v]* - to withdraw
að vera með sér *[v]* - to carry
aðgangur *[m]* - account, admission
aðstoðarflugmaður *[m]* - copilot
bakpoki *[m]* - rucksack
Bandaríkin - United States
banka reikningur *[m]* - bank account
bankastaða *[f]* - account balance
bankayfirlit *[n]* - bank statement
banki *[m]* - bank
bavían *[m]* - baboon
beint *[adj]* - direct
beint flug - nonstop
Belgía - Belgium
beltisdýr *[n]* - armadillo
bílskúr *[m]* - garage
björgunarvesti *[n]* - life preserver
björn *[m]* - bear
blettatígur *[m]* - cheetah
bókun *[f]* - booking
borð *[n]* - table
boðberi *[m]* - courier
bréf *[n]* - letter, note
bréfberi *[m]* - postman
Bretland - Great Britain
brottfararspjald *[n]* - boarding pass
brottför *[f]* - departure
dagdýr *[adj]* - diurnal
Danmörk - Denmark
debetkort *[n]* - debit card
dollarar *[mp]* - dollars
dyravörður *[m]* - doorman

dýr *[n]* - animal
dýragarðsgestur *[m]* - zoo visitor
dýragarðsvörður *[m]* - zookeeper
dýragarður *[m]* - zoo
eitraður *[adj]* - poisonous
endurgerð *[f]* - recreation
engi *[n]* - meadow
England - England
Evrópa - Europe
evrur *[fp]* - euros
eyja *[f]* - island
eyðimörk *[f]* - desert
færslur *[fp]* - transactions
farangur *[m]* - luggage
farþegi *[m]* - passenger
ferðatékki *[m]* - travellers cheque
ferðaþjónusta *[f]* - travel agency
fílagirðing *[f]* - elephant enclosure
fílahús *[n]* - elephant house
fíll *[m]* - elephant
Finnland - Finland
fjall *[n]* - mountain
fjallaljón *[n]* - cougar
fjárhæð *[f]* - amount
fjármagn *[f]* - capital
fjörður *[m]* - bay
flatlendi *[n]* - plain
fljúga *[v]* - flying
flóðhestur *[m]* - hippopotamus
flug *[n]* - flight
flugbraut *[f]* - runway
flugfreyja *[f]* - stewardess
flugmaður *[m]* - pilot
flugpóstur *[m]* - airmail
flugskýli *[n]* - hangar
flugtak *[n]* - take off
flugvél *[f]* - airplane
flugvöllur *[m]* - airport

Frakkland - France
frímerki *[n]* - postage stamp
froskdýr *[f]* - amphibian
frumskógur *[m]* - jungle
fuglasafn *[n]* - aviary
fyrsta flokks farrými *[n]* - first class
gestamóttaka *[f]* - reception desk
gestamóttakandi *[m]* - receptionist
geymsla *[f]* - vault
gíraffahús *[n]* - giraffe house
gíraffi *[m]* - giraffe
girðing *[f]* - enclosing wall
gjá *[f]* - gulf
gjald *[n]* - fee
gjaldkeri *[m]* - teller
gjaldmiðill *[m]* - currency
gjaldmiðlaskipti *[f]* - money exchanger
gjaldmiðlavirði *[n]* - exchange rate
glerbúr *[n]* - glass case
gluggi *[m]* - window
göngubrú *[f]* - gangway
gorilla *[f]* - gorilla
gras *[n]* - grass
greiðsla *[f]* - payment
Grikkland - Greece
grimmilegur *[adj]* - fierce
gróði *[m]* - profit
hægðalyf *[n]* - laxative
hættulegur *[adj]* - dangerous
hæð *[f]* - floor (storey), hill
hæð *[n]* - altitude
haf *[n]* - ocean
heimilisfang *[n]* - address
hellir *[m]* - cave
herbergi *[n]* - room
herbergisþjónusta *[f]* - room service
heyrnartól *[f]* - headphones
hitamælir *[m]* - thermometer

hjól *[n]* - wheel
hjörtur *[m]* - gazelle
hlébarði *[m]* - leopard
hlið *[n]* - gate
hlutabréf *[n]* - share
Holland - Netherlands
hotel *[n]* - hotel
hraðbanki *[m]* - ATM
hryggleysingjar *[mp]* - vertebrate
hyena *[f]* - hyena
Indland - India
innanlands *[adj]* - domestic
innflutningur *[m]* - import
inngangur *[m]* - entrance
innheimta *[f]* - invoice
innlögn *[f]* - deposit
innritun *[f]* - check-in
innspýting *[f]* - injection
insulin *[n]* - insulin
internet *[n]* - internet
Írland - Ireland
ís *[m]* - ice
Ísrael - Israel
Ítalía - Italy
jaguar *[m]* - jaguar
Japan - Japan
jarðhæð *[f]* - ground floor
jarðneskur *[adj]* - terrestrial
jarðskjálfti *[m]* - earthquake
joð *[n]* - iodine
Júgóslavía - Yugoslavia
jurtaæta *[f]* - herbivore
káeta *[f]* - cabin
Kanada - Canada
kaup *[f]* - purchase
kengúra *[f]* - kangaroo
kerra *[f]* - tray
Kína - China

klink *[n]* - coin
klósett *[n]* - toilet, loo
kóalabjörn *[m]* - koala
koddi *[m]* - pillow
koma *[f]* - arrival
kortisón *[n]* - cortisone
kreditkort *[n]* - credit card
krókódíll *[m]* - alligator, crocodile
kvörtun *[f]* - complaint
læknir *[m]* - pharmacist
lækur *[m]* - lake
lán *[n]* - loan
land *[n]* - land
landslag *[n]* - landscape
lánstraust *[n]* - credit
leigubíll *[m]* - taxi
ljón *[n]* - lion
loftræsting *[f]* - air conditioning
löggæslumaður *[m]* - officer
Lúxemborg - Luxembourg
lyf *[n]* - medicine
lyfseðill *[m]* - prescription
lyfta *[f]* - lift
lykill *[m]* - key
mamaldýr *[n]* - mammal
mammaldýr *[n]* - aardvark
matsalur *[m]* - dining room
mauraæta *[f]* - anteater
millifærsla *[f]* - funds transfer
miðasala *[f]* - ticket agent
miði *[m]* - ticket
miði aðra leið - single ticket
miði báðar leiðir - round trip ticket
morgunmatur *[m]* - breakfast
Morokkó - Morocco
móttaka *[f]* - lobby
munnskol *[n]* - dental floss
mýri *[f]* - marsh

næturdýr - nocturnal
nashyrningur *[m]* - rhinoceros
náttúra *[f]* - nature
nes *[n]* - cape
neyðar *[m]* - emergency
Noregur - Norway
Norður Ameríka - North America
núverandi aðgangur *[m]* - current account
Nýja Sjáland - New Zealand
ókyrrð *[f]* - turbulence
öryggishlið *[n]* - metal detector
öryggiskerfi *[n]* - alarm
öryggisskápur *[m]* - safe, safe deposit box
öryggisvörður *[m]* - security, guard
pakki *[m]* - package
panda *[f]* - panda
pardusdýr *[n]* - panther
peningasending *[f]* - money order
peningur *[m]* - money
pensilín *[n]* - penicillin
plástur *[m]* - bandage
Portúgal - Portugal
póstbox *[n]* - letterbox
pósthús *[n]* - post office
póstur *[m]* - post
prentað bréf *[n]* - printed item
prósenta *[f]* - percentage
rándýr *[f]* - carnivore
refur *[m]* - fox
reikningur *[m]* - bill
rúm *[n]* - bed
Rússland - Russia
sædýr *[f]* - aquatic
sædýrabúr *[n]* - aquarium
sæti *[n]* - seat
samningur *[m]* - contract
sandur *[m]* - sand
sebrahestur *[m]* - zebra

seinn *[adv]* - late
sendandi *[m]* - sender
seðill *[m]* - cash
sjávarföll *[f]* - tide
sjávarströnd *[f]* - coast
sjór *[m]* - sea
skagi *[m]* - peninsula
skilaboð *[f]* - message
skjalataska *[f]* - suitcase
skógur *[m]* - forest
Skotland - Scotland
skráð bréf *[n]* - registered letter
skriðdýr *[f]* - reptile
skriðdýragirðing *[f]* - reptile enclosure
skuld *[f]* - debt
skurður *[m]* - canal
Slóvenía - Slovenia
snemma *[adv]* - early
Spánn - Spain
sparnaðarreikningur *[m]* - savings account
sparnaður *[m]* - savings
staða *[f]* - balance
steinn *[m]* - rock, stone
stífla *[f]* - dam
stigar *[mp]* - staircase, stairs
stofa *[f]* - living room
stóll *[m]* - chair
strönd *[f]* - beach
sundlaug *[f]* - swimming pool
súrefni *[n]* - oxygen
Suður Afríka - South Africa
Suður Ameríka - South America
svalir *[m]* - balcony
svar *[n]* - reply
sveit *[f]* - countryside
Sviss - Switzerland
svíta *[f]* - suite
Svíþjóð - Sweden

sýklalyf *[n]* - antibiotic
sýróp *[n]* - syrup
tafla *[f]* - pill, tablet
tap *[n]* - loss
tegundir *[fp]* - species
tékkabók *[f]* - chequebook
tékki *[m]* - cheque
tenging *[f]* - connection
teppi *[n]* - blanket
teppi *[f]* - carpet
tígur *[m]* - tiger
tjörn *[f]* - pond
tollfrjáls *[adj]* - duty-free
trjábýll - arboreal
Túnis - Tunisia
Tyrkland - Turkey
úlfur *[m]* - wolf
umhverfi *[n]* - environment
umslag *[n]* - envelope
upplýsingar *[f]* - information
utandyra búr *[n]* - outside cage
utandyra girðing *[f]* - outdoor enclosure
útfluttningur *[m]* - export
útgangur *[m]* - exit
útgjöld *[np]* - expenses
útsýni *[n]* - view
úttekt *[f]* - withdrawal
vængur *[m]* - wing
vegabréf *[n]* - passport
verð *[n]* - price
vextir *[mp]* - interest
veðsetning *[f]* - mortgage
vikapiltur *[m]* - bellboy
virði *[n]* - value
vítamín *[n]* - vitamin
viðskiptavinur *[m]* - customer
Wales - Wales
yfirflugfreyja *[f]* - air hostess

yfirmaður *[m]* - manager
þerna *[f]* - maid
þyngd *[f]* - weight
þyrla *[f]* - helicopter
þyrlupallur *[m]* - helipad
Þýskaland - Germany

About the Author

Erik Zidowecki is a computer programmer and language lover. He is a co-founder of UniLang and founder of Parleremo, both web communities dedicated to helping people learn languages. He is also the Editor in Chief of Parrot Time magazine, a magazine devoted to language, linguistics, culture and the Parleremo community.

Made in the USA
Coppell, TX
17 June 2021